Ontario

"Partners in Progress"
by W. Robert Finegan

Pictorial Research
by Judith L. Evans

Produced in cooperation with the
Ontario Chamber of Commerce

Windsor Publications, Inc.
Chatsworth, California

Ontario

THE MODEL COLONY

An Illustrated History
by Ruth Austen

ONTARIO.

Windsor Publications, Inc.—History Books Division
Managing Editor: Karen Story
Design Director: Alexander D'Anca
Photo Director: Susan L. Wells
Executive Editor: Pamela Schroeder

Staff for *Ontario: The Model Colony*
Manuscript Editor: Jeffrey Reeves
Photo Editors: Cameron Cox, Lisa Willinger
Senior Editor, Corporate Biographies: Judith L. Hunter
Production Editor, Corporate Biographies: Albert Polito
Customer Service Manager: Phyllis Feldman-Schroeder
Editorial Assistants: Kim Kievman, Michael Nugwynne, Michelle
    Oakley, Kathy B. Peyser, Susan Schlanger, Theresa J. Solis
Publisher's Representative, Corporate Biographies:
    Allison Alan-Lee, Jennifer Olivitch
Layout Artist, Editorial: Michael Burg
Layout Artist, Corporate Biographies: Bonnie Felt
Designer: Ellen Ifrah

Windsor Publications, Inc.
Elliot Martin, Chairman of the Board
James L. Fish III, Chief Operating Officer
Michele Sylvestro, Vice President/Sales-Marketing
Mac Buhler, Vice President/Sponsor Acquisitions

Library of Congress Cataloging-in-Publication Data
Austen, Ruth.
    Ontario : the model colony : an illustrated history / by Ruth Austen
    : Partners in progress by W. Robert Finegan
    p.   cm.
    "Produced in cooperation with the Ontario Chamber of Commerce."
    Includes bibliographical references.
    ISBN: 0-89781-349-9
    1. Ontario—History. 2. Ontario—Description and travel—Views.
3. Ontario—Industries. I. Title.
F1058.A97   1990   90-31270
971.3—dc20   CIP

FRONTISPIECE: The Bancroft Company of San Francisco produced this impressive lithograph showing Ontario in its infancy, less than one year after its founding. Courtesy, Ontario City Library, Model Colony History Room

Contents

Acknowledgments

A number of people helped wholeheartedly with this project. First and foremost, there was Judy Evans, librarian for the Ontario City Library's Model Colony History Room. Judy's knowledge of Ontario history, her instant recall, and her cheerful support were the infrastructure of the research for this book. La Vera Miller and George May, who also work in the Model Colony History Room, spent many hours helping me locate obscure information. My research assistant, Ty Slyder, University of California, Riverside, graduate student in history, compiled a chronology which will be of benefit to Ontario history researchers well beyond the scope of this book. I had other research assistance from Glenn Williams, a former student of mine, and Ellen Koehler, my daughter. Harry Lawton, whose local history expertise is legendary, held long conversations with me on the nuances of producing a history. My editor at Windsor, Jeffrey Reeves, put the polish on this manuscript with a caring and delicate touch. My deepest thanks and appreciation, Jeffrey. My final words of gratitude, however, go to two women who died this year--my mother and my grandmother. Mary E. Noland and Sarah E. Wintermeyer always had unfailing faith in me as a writer.

Once Ontario incorporated in 1891, city services, such as the sanitation department, shown here in an image from around 1920, were established. Courtesy, Ontario City Library, Model Colony History Room

Prologue

"It is a sunny morning in the Fall of 1882. A solitary figure is standing on the mesa at the head of the plain lying between the flood-water washes of the Cucamonga Canyon on the east and the San Antonio Canyon the west. He is a heavily-bearded man of thirty-four, slightly above medium height, who stands long gazing with thoughtful blue eyes down the narrow rectangle of dusty, whitish-brown country extending directly in front of him from the foot of the Sierra Madre Range. The tract in which he is so interested is about seven miles long, running from north to south, and varies from a mile to three miles wide, east and west. The plain beginning at his feet is a slightly inclined plane, falling in a continuous slope to the horizon, where blue sky and purple sage brush merge and melt into one. There is not one human habitation visible—for ages jack rabbit and coyote have had it to themselves. After the infrequent rains it is covered with evanescent wild flowers, but in its normal arid state only sage bursh and a few other desert growths can retain a footing there. So this lovely slope lying at the foot of snow-capped Old Baldy is useless for cultivation unless water can be brought from the mountains.

"The watcher long stands motionless drinking in, not the calm beauty of the valley nor the lofty grandeur of the Sierra Madres, but the charm of a scene which lies before him in imagination only. He is dreaming a dream which shall come true. He sees lying at his feet a colony settled by prosperous people setting a standard of comfort formerly deemed unattainable by ordinary people, extracting a generous living from a soil thought by generations of Spanish proprietors to be incapable of settlement. It is at once a Rus in Urbe and an Urbs in Rure, where the best features of town and country life have been retained. It is a rustic retreat without loneliness, a city without slums or saloons. He sees this imaginary colony bisected by a noble avenue (now one of the most celebrated thoroughfares in America) planted with a quadruple row of trees extending some seven miles in a straight line down the slope. He sees in the heart of this dream city a famous school (which will owe to him its existence and its munificent endowment), the pride and admiration of the far-flung educational district of which it will become the Alma Mater. He sees a colony bearing the euphonious name of his native Canadian

One of George Chaffey's first projects was planning and laying out Euclid Avenue. This view, taken around 1886, shows telephone poles running up the center of the avenue connecting the land office with Etiwanda. Chaffey named the avenue after the ancient Greek mathematician Euclid. Courtesy, Ontario City Library, Model Colony History Room

province, regarded by the people of the Americas as a model of the soundest principles of irrigation settlement and social organization—a city beautiful, bathed in perpetual sunshine. Directly above it the hoary head of Old Baldy, then a thousand feet high, pierces the clouds which sluter lovingly around, Nature and Man thus combining to make this one of the most lovely spots ever selected for human habitation.

"George Chaffey, for the solitary watcher on the mesa was he, saw all this in a golden vision on the morning late in the year 1882, from which the history of Ontario dates. He had conceived the plan of buying the Cucamonga and Kincaid ranches with the object of planting on them a colony which should surpass any-

thing of the kind yet attempted in California. He arranged to spend the morning alone on a spot from which he could see the whole of his new domain, and there he worked out the main features of the new settlement of Ontario. To use his own words to the writer exactly forty-four years later: 'From the plateau at the foot of the mountain I obtained a bird's-eye view of the whole area I proposed to acquire, and while I was standing there looking at it, I saw what Ontario was to and did become.' "

From *The Life of George Chaffey: A Story of Irrigation Beginning in California and Australia* by J.A. Alexander, Copyright 1928. Reprinted by permission of Macmillan and Co. Ltd.

*Ferdinand Deppe's 1832 painting of the Mission
San Gabriel Arcangel shows a thatched Indian house
in the foreground and a Corpus Christi procession
in front of the mission. The Gabrielinos Indians,
local to the Ontario area, were so named by the Franciscan fathers because of their proximity to the mission where many of the Indians worked. From,
"Franciscan Friars of California," courtesy, Mission
Santa Barbara Archive-Library*

The Land is Settled

Ontario is located on the San Bernardino Plain about 50 miles east of Los Angeles and 20 miles west of San Bernardino. The plain is an expanse of sand, gravel, and boulders that looks as if it were poured from the San Gabriel Mountains to the north in one huge sheet. In a sense, it was. Dominating the valley above Ontario and its surroundings are Mt. San Antonio ("Old Baldy") and Cucamonga and Ontario peaks. Cucamonga Peak is visibly flat on top. That flatness represents sections of the original valley floor. Loose dirt, gravel, and rocks flow very swiftly from the still forming slopes of these young mountains with the sometimes torrential rains.

Valley and plain have taken more than 10 million years to form, and in simple terms, one block of ground rose as another sank. Geologists have placed the beginning of the area's geologic history at the time estimated for the formation of the San Andreas Fault—between 12 and 28 million years ago. The San Gabriel Mountains are part of the unusual east-west trending Transverse Ranges, which run across the generally north-south grain of Southern California. The San Gabriels are intersected some 25 miles east of Ontario at Cajon Pass by the San Andreas Fault. They were partially formed by geologic activity along this highly active fault as well as by the up-and-down fault-block action responsible for forming the entire Transverse province.

Visible to the south of Ontario, and occasionally capped with snow, is a portion of the Peninsular Range, consisting of the Santa Ana Mountains, the base of which is carved deeply by the Santa Ana River. Several blocks of the Peninsular Range are separated by faults also generally attributed to the San Andreas fault system.

Small rolling hills make up the northwest portion of the valley—the Chino Hills, Diamond Bar, and the Covina Hills—and teem with lacy fish fossils preserved in soft mudstone matrices. Around 10 million years ago this area was a tropical lagoon edged by a small active volcano located near the modern-day Puddingstone Reservoir in the hills above Pomona.

The Transverse and Peninsular ranges meet in the San Gorgonio Pass area, 50 miles east of Ontario. Mt. San Gorgonio ("Old Grayback"), the tallest peak in Southern California, dominates these ranges and is frequently visible to Ontario area residents.

Each time the earth shakes from movement along any of the many faults related to the formation of Ontario's surrounding mountains, the forces that went into making this land become evident.

Wind, Fire, and Water—The Climate
Ontario is at its most spectacular during the winter months. The nearly flat alluvial plain on which it is located is rimmed by snow-capped mountains. Atmospheric conditions conspire to make the air so dry that depth perception nearly disappears. A mountain that is more than 10 miles away seems to be only at arm's length. On a particularly spectacular winter evening, all the mountains in sight—from the nearby San Gabriels to the faraway peaks of San Gorgonio and San Jacinto—have snow blankets. The air is clear; to the west the setting sun sends a reddish glow to the white mountaintops, where wind whips the powder snow hundreds of feet into the air,

ABOVE: Dashing vaqueros round up cattle, live-stock that provided the most profit for rancheros in the mid-1700s. Courtesy, University of California Extension Media Center, Berkeley

RIGHT: This stone marker in De Anza Park commemorates the expedition of Juan Bautista de Anza in 1774. It is thought that Anza and his group camped near this spot during their journey to Monterey. The marker was placed here by the Boy Scouts on February 8, 1930. Courtesy, Ontario City Library, Model Colony History Room

and in the east a full moon rises. Winter rains will turn the sun-browned chaparral into a sea of green, and in late winter and early spring blankets of blue, orange, red, and yellow wildflowers cover the alluvium and lower mountain slopes as the pungent and sweet smells of blooming buckwheat and sage fill the air. Briefly, the land hints at its presettlement state before trees were cut for fencing and firewood, cattle and sheep grazed the region nearly bare, and watershed in the mountains was cut and burned.

When early Spanish explorers came to the area, the land demonstrated a lushness that lasted year-round and would have surprised those who founded Ontario a little more than 100 years later. In Ingersoll's *Century Annals of San Bernardino County 1769-1904*, Ontario colonist Eleanor Freeman wrote:

In the winter of 1882, what is now the town and colony of Ontario was a barren waste extending from the San Antonio Canon on the north to the Rancho Santa Ana del Chino on the south and from Cucamonga on the east to Rancho San Jose on the west. No vegetation but sage brush covered these plains, even the Indians had not found them good hunting grounds and they had been left to the jack rabbit and the coyote.

On March 21, 1774, the first expedition of Juan Bautista de Anza, seeking an inland route from Sonora to Monterey, camped on San Antonio Creek near what is now De Anza Park at the corner of Euclid Avenue and Phillips Street in Ontario. The previous day the company had swung through Moreno Valley, then crossed Riverside to camp on the Santa Ana River somewhere below Mount Rubidoux, about 20 miles from San Antonio Creek. The party had to construct a bridge in order to cross the Santa Ana.

Compare Anza's impression of the terrain around Ontario with that of Freeman:

Having taken our train by the little bridge, at half past eight in the morning we set forth west northwest, over good country covered with pasturage, the Sierra Nevada continuing on our right. After going about seven leagues we halted for the night at a fertile arroyo which came from this sierra, and was thickly grown with cottonwoods, willows and sycamores. It was given the name of Los Osos, because of several bears which were seen here and then ran away.

Another of the company's diarists commented on the snow-covered mountains, good pasturage, and "many deer of different species were seen pasturing in the fields."

Tall sycamores, their large broad leaves rattling in the wind, forests of oaks on the hillsides, cottonwoods, alders, and willows along the creeks and streams accented the otherwise low-lying plant life. The occasional and often seasonal creeks flowed in cut gullies. San Antonio Creek, variously called Arroyo de los Alisos (sycamores) and Arroyo de los Osos was a fair-sized, year-round stream with cold, crystal-clear water that issued from nearby San Antonio Canyon and fed into the Santa Ana River. Along the foothills, artesian springs flowed most of the year, marking the fault lines.

Not only did the fault system create the backdrop, but its work eventually affected the climate. As the mountains rose, air flow across the area changed, water systems changed, rivers were born, and erosion from the rains contributed to situations where one drainage system robbed another of its water.

The climate on the San Bernardino plain is considered to be Mediterranean. It is technically a high desert, generally arid, with an average rainfall of 10 to 24 inches a year. Possibly the first reference to the Mediterranean climate was made in 1776 by Father Pedro Font on the second Anza expedition through the region. His entry was made the day the Anza party left the

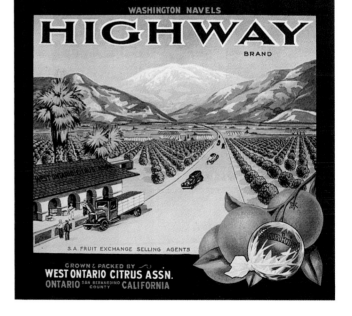

Ontario's involvement in the citrus industry dates
back to the late 1800s. In describing the first orange labels from the town, the Ontario Record said they
were "decidedly neat if not gaudy....Grown and
packed at Ontario, California is among the prominent display lines." Courtesy, Floyd J. McDonald

camp on San Antonio Creek, by then re-named from Arroyo de los Osos to Arroyo de los Alisos. Though he described the area around what is now San Dimas, sev-eral miles west of Ontario, the entire plain was much the same:

. . . Then one enters a country very level in all directions, which we found very green in places, the flowers already bursting into bloom. The earth is very moist, not only because here the rainy season is in the winter as in Spain, but also because of the great fogs which I have noticed falling in the night when it is fair. The rains are fine, gentle, and continuous, and without thunder. In some places live oaks are seen, and apparently in the sierra there are more of them together with the pines . . .

The date of this entry was Wednesday, Janu-ary 3, 1776. Before he left the campsite in Ontario, Font noted a carving on a large sycamore made by Anza in 1774, "I H S," and added: "In the year of 1776 came the San Francisco expedition." No one knows when that ancient tree fell.

Around Ontario, as in the rest of the valley, temperatures only occassionally reach freezing in the winter but often soar into the 100s during the summer months. The area's climate, however, has its vaga-ries, with times of extreme drought and ex-treme flooding. It is one of the ironies of Southern California that the greatest floods seem to follow the greatest droughts and fires.

Air in the basin is dry and generally clear except when the area's natural mists and hazes, noted by Father Font, cut down on visibility. Fogs invade the valley from the ocean beaches during the fall and spring with the seasonal cooling and warm-ing of the Pacific Ocean. They do not burn off easily. The basin's mountain ranges form a bowl that acts as a trap for smoke from brush and forest fires and modern-day air pollution, particularly during the hot summer months. During

the early years of the citrus industry, residents choked on oily smoke from smudge pots that were lit during the infrequent freezes to protect the frost-sensitive fruit. Modern Southern Califor-nians have no monopoly on creating eye-stinging air pollution.

Winds periodically come funneling through the mountain passes with gusts between 35 and 45 miles per hour, and at times up to 100 miles per hour. The winds pick up tons of dirt that literally sandblast shrubs, trees, and land alike. One of the first mentions of these winds was in Richard H. Dana's *Three Years Before The Mast*: "Saturday, February 13, 1836. We were called up at midnight to slip for a violent northeaster, for this miserable hole of San Pedro is thought unsafe in almost every wind." Though the ship successfully sought refuge off Catalina Island for that storm, later it was blown off course and sent skittering halfway to Hawaii with its sails stripped from the yards.

Early rancho residents along the Santa Ana River thought the winds were formed through the Santa Ana Canyon. Though technically a misnomer, they are still called Santa Ana winds. At the right time of year, they move thousands of tumbleweeds across the valley floor. Often the Santa Anas drive cataclysmic fires across the land.

While fire is highly destructive to man-made structures, Southern California's na-tive plant system evolved to survive it. In fact, many of the plants cannot reseed un-less the seed pods are first burned. Others need the wind to help spread their seeds. Both fire and floods clear away debris to make room for younger and healthier plants.

Water erosion is extreme in this gener-ally rising plain. In 1772 Spanish explorer Pedro Fages commented on the apparent flatness of the land as he first viewed it from a rise near Cajon Pass. "The moun-tains, the river, and the hills all seem familiar in their main outline, but in closer inspection we see differences in detail. So little of the land is level! It is a crisscross of gullies, ravines, hills and slopes," he wrote.

In 1825 a flood altered the Santa Ana River bed so that it flowed into the Pacific several miles from its prior entry point. The 1856-1864 drought, which ravaged livestock on the early ranches, leaving the bones of hundreds of thousands of beef cattle bleaching in the sun, included a flood of epic proportions in the winter of 1861-1862. Twenty years later a record rainfall of 36.5 inches fell on the San Bernardino Plain. On March 6, 1884, the billowing waters wiped out newly installed railroad lines and once again altered the Santa Ana River course.

Water carved the land, established channels still followed today in flood control efforts, and created its own debris basins. And the land had its own water disposal methods. It flowed to the sea or settled into the ground to enter the aquifer for future use by farmers and settlers.

Life on the Plain

The first people to arrive in the area were among the earliest inhabitants of the continent. The area supported mammoths, giant sloths, camels, ancient horses, and saber-toothed tigers. The people were big-game hunters, using spears and throwing sticks as weapons. Evidence of these people's lifestyle exists in the San Bernardino plain in the form of spear- and scraper-scarred mammoth bones unearthed in gravel pits.

Better archaeological documentation exists for the second wave of human migration into the region, which started 8,000 years ago. These people appear to have been more oriented to plant food sources than their predecessors. Though the groups of inhabitants changed from time to time, the lifestyle remained much the same, as it was dictated by climate and availability of food.

Linguistic evidence indicates that people of the Hokan language group lived in the region prior to A.D. 500. They were gradually pushed out, to the north and the south, by Shoshonean language groups migrating from the Great Basin region.

There is no way of knowing what these people called themselves, or even how many there were prior to the introduction of European diseases as early as 1542. By the time the Spanish missionaries arrived, it is believed the Indians' culture had already suffered greatly. Certainly their numbers had.

The people who made their home and found a livelihood in the Ontario area immediately prior to and during the Mission Period are today referred to as Gabrielinos, after the Mission San Gabriel. The geographic area occupied by this group included the Channel Islands, coastal Orange and Los Angeles counties, the Los Angeles Basin, and the valleys of western San Bernardino and Riverside counties.

Father Jose Maria Zalvidea, traveling from Cajon Pass to the Mission San Gabriel in 1806, noted that an Indian rancheria by the name of Guapiana was located on San Antonio Creek near present day Ontario. If it is the same rancheria listed in San Gabriel Mission records variously as Guapiabit, Guapian, Apiambit, and Apiagma, it was a good-size village because 89 converts came from there between the years 1795 and 1815.

One nearby village was Cucamongabit, located near the site of a large *cienaga* (swamp) fed by springs. The modern-day city of Rancho Cucamonga is located at exactly the same spot. Other large villages were Totabit, located near the current Prado Dam site, and Toybipet, in Claremont.

According to Hugo Reid, a California pioneer from Scotland who married a Gabrielino woman, the Indians

. . . *comprised one great Family under distinct Chiefs. They spoke nearly the same language, with the exception of a few words . . . Being related by blood and marriage, war was never carried on between them. When war was consequently waged against neighboring tribes of no affinity, it was a common cause.*

Like most people, they worried about wrinkling in old age and balding. Women wore red ochre to ward off the effects of sun and wind, while special charcoal pastes were applied to the scalp twice a day to restore hair growth. Tattooing was an important part of body adornment. Both men and women wore their hair long. Men parted theirs in the middle, either braided or pinned up. Women wore theirs long and garlanded with flowers. They bathed daily before sunrise and dried out at the breakfast fire.

Men and children went without clothes in the summer months, and during the rain and cold wore robes made of rabbit- and deerskin. Women wore aprons of woven plants and strips of fur. Ritual costumes made of woven skins, plumage from different birds, shells, and beads, and which were worn during dances, were the most colorful clothing.

The Gabrielinos were great traders, storytellers, and artisans, living in large

This mural by Charles R. Knight portrays the huge ground sloths, saber-toothed tigers, vultures, and giant mastodons known to roam the San Gabriel Valley during the prehistoric age. Courtesy, Los Angeles County Museum of Natural History

semipermanent villages surrounded by a number of smaller, usually temporary, settlements for the purposes of hunting, fishing, and gathering of seasonal plant foods.

A favorite food, Reid wrote, was "the large locust or grasshopper . . . roasted on a stick at the fire." They also hunted deer, coyotes, squirrels, badgers, rats, gophers, snakes, raccoons, skunks, wildcats, crows, and other birds, including hawks and burrowing owls. The men and boys fished the streams using lines and hooks, nets, basket traps, and poisons derived from plants. They also hunted with bows and arrows and spears, and trapped with deadfalls and snares.

The indigenous chaparral is a rich source of edible plants, and the native people made use of them all. The women collected acorns, seeds, and fruits in huge quantities for preparation and storage. Early Ontario pioneers plowed up great numbers of their grinding stones and bowls. Foodstuffs included acorns, buckwheat, bitter cherry, toyon, yucca, yerba santa, cat's claw, penstemon, sagebrush, sage, laurel sumac, mesquite, and barberry.

Besides plants used for food, there were a number of medicinal and ritual plants, including white sage, calabazilla, jimson weed (datura), and tobacco. Wil-

square miles) each. By 1848, when California became part of the United States under the Treaty of Guadalupe Hidalgo, more than 800 of these ranchos had been apportioned. The impact that the formation of the ranchos had on the culture of California has lasted, especially in Southern California, to this day. The rancho lifestyle continued well after the United States acquired California from Mexico in 1848. It was the age of the dashing *rancheros* who never rode a horse at less than a dead run—the rancheros who became the first of the cattle barons and who had such great influence over the state's commercial and shipping interests. It is their Spanish surnames that appear on so many modern-day towns, parks, and streets. These were the *Californios*, many of whom were descendants of the first Spanish soldiers and settlers.

In his book *Ranchos of California*, Robert G. Cowan describes the Californios as

. . . well favored in physique and appearance. The men were tall, muscular and athletic, and the women were attractive and rather small. Their dress was picturesque and colorful. No matter how poor, the don had the bearing of a grandee, and wore clothes to match. He might have only one suit, and that worn thread bare, but it was worn with great dignity. The style of dress was subject to continual change, but throughout the pastoral period the men's raiment was more colorful than was the women's.

Tiburcio Tapia was among the Californios who obtained one of the coveted grants. On March 3, 1839, Governor Juan B. Alvarado awarded him a tract of land that included Ontario, Upland, Etiwanda, Cucamonga, and parts of Colton and Fontana. Possession of a land grant was dependent upon a survey. Competition for the land was fierce, and Tapia's surveying party included neighboring rancho owners Juan Bandini of Rancho Jurupa and Ygnacio Palomares of Rancho San Jose (now

Pomona), who wanted to make sure their lands were not encroached upon. The official surveyors were accompanied by assistants and the *cordeleros* (cord bearers). The land was measured with knotted rawhide cords 209 *varas* (about 192 yards) long with stakes attached at each end. On horseback, the cordeleros carried the cords from one point to the next.

It must have been a hard-riding party that set out in February to survey the Rancho Cucamonga lands. Moving as fast as the assistants could record, over a period of several days seven square leagues (about 21 square miles) of the San Bernardino Valley were measured off for Tapia's use.

Tapia employed Indians to lay out his vineyard and build the adobe house on Red Hill. They herded the cattle along San Antonio Creek, further exposing to erosion the ground that would become Ontario. Gradually, the Indians were replaced by Mexican laborers, and the natives retreated to the hills and canyons, joining the ranks of the raiders.

Tapia lived on his rancho until 1845, when he died during a trip to Los Angeles. It is conjectured that poison he was using to get rid of coyotes remained beneath his fingernails, and he inadvertently poisoned himself while eating.

After Tapia's death the estate went to his daughter, Maria Merced Tapia, who went to live with her godmother while the land was managed by a majordomo. On July 4, 1847, she married French trapper Leon Victor Prudhomme, who then took over management of the rancho.

One other land-grant parcel and its owners played a significant part in Ontario history. In 1841 the Rancho Santa Ana del Chino was deeded to Antonio Maria Lugo, one of the most influential and wealthy of the Californios. On December 24, 1836, his 13-year-old daughter, Maria de Jesus Lugo, married Isaac J. Williams, a fur trapper and native of Pennsylvania.

Lugo gave his new son-in-law 4,000

Maria Merced Williams was the daughter of Isaac Williams, owner of the Santa Ana del Chino Rancho. On September 16, 1856, she married John Rains at the Plaza Church in Los Angeles. After the death of Rains in 1862 Maria Merced, or the Dona Merced as she came to be known, struggled to maintain the Rancho Cucamonga. She eventually lost the property through foreclosure and moved to Los Angeles to live with her daughter. Courtesy, Casa de Rancho Cucamonga Historical Society

In 1858 John Rains, a former sub-agent at Temecula for the San Luis Rey Indians, purchased the Cucamonga Rancho from Victor Prudhomme for approximately $8,500. Rains would eventually build the house that is now the home of the Casa de Rancho Cucamonga Historical Society. Courtesy, Casa de Rancho Cucamonga Historical Society

head of cattle and the 22,000-acre Chino ranch. Within four years Williams had added 13,000 acres to the property, and he eventually became one of the most powerful cattle barons in California. Williams' second child, Maria Merced Williams (later known as Doña Merced), married adventurer John Rains in 1856, when she was 17. Rains bought the Rancho del Cucamonga from Tiburcio Tapia's daughter, Maria Merced Tapia de Prudhomme, and the son-in-law Tapia never met, Victor L. Prudhomme, on July 22, 1858.

John Rains was killed in an ambush on November 17, 1862, leaving the property in financial disarray. Though suspicion fell on several of Rains' alleged enemies, no one was ever brought to trial for the murder. Maria Merced was granted title in 1863, and eventually the bulk of the rancho was broken up with the foreclosure forced by Isais W. Hellman in 1871. The house itself passed back to Doña Merced in 1870.

Americans Discover California
Among the events setting the stage for the next era of development and population explosion were the Mexican-American War, which lasted from 1846 until 1848, the California Gold Rush of 1849, the floods and subsequent drought, beginning in 1861, and the decades-long effort, beginning in 1850, to build a railroad across the continent.

Prior to the Mexican War, the area around Pomona, Chino, and Cucamonga, which included the pastoral land that would one day become Ontario, was settled in a series of sprawling ranchos held by a mix of native Californios descended from native and Spanish settlers and American adventurers who had either purchased their land from the rancheros or married into their holdings. The relatively peaceful lifestyle was punctuated by an occasional Indian raid, usually followed by a counter-raid on the Indians by groups of hot-headed sons of rancheros.

On July 7, 1846, this lifestyle was permanently disrupted when the California capitol at Monterey was captured by the United States Pacific Squadron under the command of Commodore Robert F. Stockton. The Mexican government, along with the Californios, retaliated, and the ensuing war lasted until 1848 when Mexico ceded California, among other territories, to the United States with the signing of the Treaty of Guadalupe Hidalgo. Two years later California was admitted to the Union as the 31st state.

The Gold Rush of 1849, which began with the discovery of gold in a Northern California stream at Sutter's Mill, not only brought in thousands of new residents to the new state, but also led to the establishment of a unique California civilization. Both Los Angeles and San Francisco became urbanized, thanks to the sudden influx of people from all walks of life.

The cattle ranchers of Southern California thrived on the Gold Rush, driving herds of rangy Mexican cattle north each year where they were sold for about $25 a head. This period of economic boom ended abruptly for the ranchers with the severe floods of 1861, followed by two years of drought that left, among others, the land of Rancho Cucamonga and Rancho Santa Ana del Chino a virtual desert.

Adroit supervision on the part of Robert Carlisle, the man who managed Rancho Cucamonga after the death of John Rains, saved the bulk of that rancho's cattle from becoming part of the Southern California boneyard. The rest of the region, however, was devastated. Some ranchos were left without a single surviving steer, and most rancheros were forced into bankruptcy. In addition, the demand for the lean Mexican cattle diminished as better breeds of beef cattle were introduced into the northern part of the state. Southern California ranchers, stuck with their herds of tough beasts, couldn't

compete. The old ranchos went into foreclosure or were sold to the first bidder.

After California was admitted to the Union in 1850, the effort to run a railroad from coast to coast gained momentum. At the time, with the states split north and south by the political and economic problems that would lead to the Civil War, Congress couldn't agree on the route.

Instead, Congress, acknowledging the need for some sort of coast-to-coast transportation and communications system, passed an appropriation for an overland mail service. John Butterfield's company in New York won the contract. The Butterfield stage line began in St. Louis, crossed through Arkansas, Texas, New Mexico, and Arizona, and passed, by way of Los Angeles, through California's Central Valley to San Francisco.

The route from Arizona was over the Santa Fe Trail, which connected eventually to the El Camino Real, and Cucamonga housed one of the stage stops. The four-horse Concord coaches regularly thundered through the future site of Ontario to cross San Antonio Creek on the way to Los Angeles.

The promise of a railroad was enough to encourage land speculation along the five routes originally surveyed in 1853. Eventually, at Promontory, Utah, on May 10, 1869, the transcontinental railroad connecting California with the rest of the country became a reality.

Now a new breed of pioneer was about to invade the San Bernardino Valley and displace, once and for all, the remnants of the great Mexican ranchos. These new settlers were Victorians, with visions of Eden-like utopias.

Cattle ranching has been a part of Ontario's history since the mission period of the late 1700s. Cattle are being branded on the Chino Ranch in this photo from the 1880s. Courtesy, Ontario City Library, Model Colony History Room

Abraham Oakley built this home on Euclid Avenue in 1887, surrounded by his 10-acre orange grove. The house is still standing today and the small palm in the center of the photo now towers many feet above the roof-line of the house. In 1987 the house received a Preservation Award from the Ontario Historic Landmarks Society. Courtesy, Ontario City Library, Model Colony History Room

The Colonial Movement

One of the most dynamic of the Victorian settlers was George B. Chaffey, Jr., who in partnership with his brother, William Benjamin Chaffey, founded Ontario. Chaffey, born in 1848 in Brockville, Canada, was the inveterate entrepreneur, establishing revolutionary irrigation systems wherever he went and then moving on to the next challenge, leaving more staid personalities to carry on with what he started.

The Chaffey family's heritage stretches back into English history with a long and honorable record of serving their country and the crown. The Canadian branch of the family was founded by Benjamin Chaffey, Jr., who came to Lake Ontario, Canada, from Stoke-sub-Handon, County of Somerset, shortly after the war of 1812. Benjamin was brother to George B. Chaffey, Sr., father of the founder of Ontario, California.

It was from this uncle, who was the engineer and the co-builder of the famous Victoria Bridge over the St. Lawrence River at Montreal, that Chaffey acquired his interest and skill in engineering.

Too impatient, too curious, and too easily bored to stick with the regular school curriculum, Chaffey always wanted to explore the next idea. Mathematics was one of his favorite pursuits; he studied and read voraciously. He went to work for his father and in his teens was given command of one of the lake tugs, and before he reached 21 he earned a master's and engineer's ticket, which allowed him to captain his father's lake-going freighters. Challenged to increase the speed of the shallow and somewhat sluggish ships, he designed a propeller that increased ship speed without increasing fuel output. Chaffey also designed passenger and freight ships for the lake trade.

In 1878, when George Chaffey was an established career man in the shipping industry, his father retired. Dr. Joseph Jarvis, a neighbor and the brother of William Chaffey's wife, visited Riverside, California, and liking what he saw, eagerly purchased a plot of land. Upon his return to Kingston, his enthusiasm about Riverside lured the Chaffey family to join him in his emigration.

In 1880 George Chaffey, who, according to his biographer J.A. Alexander, was "excited by the strange enthusiasm of his father and brother for a land so different from their beloved Canada," arrived in Southern California. He never returned to Canada. He and another Kingstonian, jeweler Matthew Gage, became fascinated with the challenge of irrigation in a land so dry. Gage built the Gage Canal in what is now Riverside County to bring water through the City of Riverside.

George B. Chaffey, Jr., went on to found two California cities, Etiwanda and Ontario, and two Australian cities, Mildura and Renmark. He also established the irrigation system for the Imperial Valley. With his Etiwanda project, Chaffey became the first person west of the Rocky Mountains to harness water power to make electricity, and his Etiwanda home was the first in Southern California to have electric incandescent lamps.

Etiwanda

During Chaffey's sojourn in Riverside, he and his brother William, a horticulturist and soil expert, toured the surrounding area. Chaffey was exploring the possibility of investments. He was also bursting with ideas.

Appalled at the confusion over water rights he saw his father and friends dealing with in Riverside, he, his brother, and L. M. Holt, editor of the *Riverside Press and Horticulturist*, worked out an idea that ultimately revolutionized the antiquated and unworkable riparian law inherited from England. Under that system, each land owner who had a claim to water simply dug a ditch to his property. Those downstream often had to resort to taking legal action in order to get their fair share.

Alexander describes the new plan as it was instituted in Etiwanda:

Stripped of technicalities, the idea was: A water company was organized, its stock consisting of one share for every acre of land comprised in the colony. Each purchaser of land received one share in the water company for every acre of land held. The water rights were sold to the water company by the vendors, the Chaffey Brothers, who had, of course, purchased the water rights with the property. They received in return for the water rights all the shares in the water company, these to be transferred pro rata to the purchasers of land. Thus ten shares in the water company would be transferred to the purchaser of each ten-acre lot. The effect of this was that the water company would assume responsibility for the distribution of water to each ten-acre tract, irrespective of nearer or remoter location, and no one was entitled to more than his proportionate share.

Both the Etiwanda and Ontario colonies were founded in 1882 under similar principles. Chaffey began the Etiwanda project in 1881 with a visit to Captain J.S. Garcia, a retired seaman whose sheep ranch occupied land the Chaffey brothers believed could be easily irrigated and turned into orchards. Located near the intersection of the El Camino Real and the Santa Fe Trail, the Garcia home was considered to be something of an oasis to hot and weary travelers.

Chaffey chose the Etiwanda site for his first colonizing experiment in part be-cause Garcia's own dabbling in irrigation already demonstrated the practicality of his scheme. Garcia planted the first orange groves in the area as well as a small vineyard and some alfalfa fields. Furthermore, William Chaffey assured his brother that the quality of the soil was ideal for subdivision into small, productive orchards for individual families. As another incentive, water flowed freely from three canyons at the base of the mountain range, and Garcia had acquired the water rights when he acquired his property.

On Thanksgiving Day in 1881 the two brothers called on Garcia. With them was surveyor John C. Dunlap of San Bernardino. The trio arrived in time to sit down for dinner. After the meal they went off to explore Day, Young, and Middle canyons. Chaffey immediately made an offer of $30,000 for 560 acres of land, water rights, and the house. The deed was signed on January 10, 1882. A month later, to bring the property up to a full section of 640 acres, Garcia accepted $1 for an additional 80 acres.

By the time the project was underway, Chaffey had 1,000 acres subdivided into 10-acre lots. According to Alexander, by 1888 the colony consisted of 2,500 acres, and Etiwanda was named for a well known Algonquin Indian chief, an old friend of the Chaffey family.

The Garcia house was George Chaffey's first home in California, and he used it as a guest house for potential investors until a hotel was built in 1883. He also used the house as the subject of experiments to satisfy his scientific curiosity and his engineer's instincts for invention. He had met Alexander Graham Bell, and certainly knew of the work of Thomas Alva Edison, and was eager to put their ideas to work.

Etiwanda was the site of the first hydroelectric current in the western United States. The water flow from his irrigation project—wooden flumes carried water from the main streams to a reservoir from which water was carried to the highest

In 1880 George Chaffey left his job in Canada to join his family in the colony of Riverside. By the end of 1882, he and his younger brother William had founded the new colony of Ontario. Four years later the brothers left for Australia where they founded two more agricultural colonies. Courtesy, Ontario City Library, Model Colony History Room

While in Riverside the Chaffey brothers became acquainted with Luther M. Holt, editor of the local newspaper. Holt was instrumental in setting up Etiwanda's mutual water company, an idea which revolutionized riparian law in the West. From Illustrated History of Southern California, *1890*

corner of each 10-acre plot—powered an 18-inch turbine. The turbine drove a dynamo to light two 3,000-candlepower arc lights at the house, which could be seen in Riverside, and aroused statewide interest.

Chaffey wired his new house himself and installed some of Edison's newly developed incandescent lamps. He also installed the first long-distance telephone line in the world, connecting Etiwanda to Riverside, San Bernardino, Colton, Redlands, and the settlement of Lugonia near Redlands.

Los Angeles was unwilling to let a small colony outshine it, so to speak, and expressed an interest in the new lighting method. George Chaffey quickly formed the Los Angeles Electric Company in 1882, at the same time he was developing plans for the Ontario colony. Because of Chaffey's work, Los Angeles became one of the first cities in the world to be lighted by electricity.

The Model Colony

By the time Ontario was platted, an agricultural precedent had been more than established in the San Bernardino Valley. In fact, the entire valley experienced a land boom, thanks to the coming of the railroad.

In 1881 Richard Gird obtained the vast Rancho Santa Ana del Chino. With visions of restoring the land to fertility after years of depredation from cattle and sheep ranching, he platted the town of Chino. Gird put in a narrow gauge railroad between Chino and Ontario, built schools, established a newspaper, the *Chino Champion*, and constructed an opera house.

Within 10 years of the development of Ontario, the towns of Lordsburg (later renamed La Verne) and Claremont—both northwest of Ontario—were also laid out.

Oranges had been planted as early as 1850 in parts of what would eventually be San Bernardino and Riverside counties. In the Riverside colony, George Chaffey's father, George Chaffey, Sr., already owned a citrus grove. Shortly after acquiring Rancho

Cucamonga, Tiburcio Tapia had put in grapevines and built a small winery. Later, John Rains expanded the vineyard and winemaking operations. When George Chaffey purchased that portion of the old rancho from Captain Garcia, he acquired those operations and expanded them with the help of German immigrant John Klusman.

Ontario is Founded

"It is said that the plan of the Chaffey Brothers for their new colony of Ontario, named for their former home in Ontario, Canada, was the most perfect then formulated for colonization," reports Ontario pioneer Eleanor Freeman in 1904 in Ingersoll's *Century Annals of San Bernardino County.*

In 1929, three years before his death at the age of 84, George Chaffey told history student Beatrice Parson Lee that he and his brother learned that "portions of the Cucamonga Rancho lying between the Arroyo San Antonio and the Arroyo Cucamonga might be purchased from the Cucamonga Land Company." She quotes him as saying, "We came over here . . . drove up to the top of the Mesa and looked over the thing. We concluded that it could be made into a very fine place."

The two Chaffeys made an offer to Captain Garcia. When the developers of the City of Pomona learned of the Chaffey brothers' efforts to acquire the San Antonio Canyon lands and water rights, they became incensed. Pomona needed the water in order to keep up with its own expansion and agricultural concerns. The fierce bidding over the San Antonio Canyon lands was the first of many competitive clashes the two cities would have over the years.

Pomona interests made a counter offer through M.L. Wicks and the Reverend Cyrus Mills, the founder of Mills College. George Chaffey immediately replied, offering an equal amount for the purchase option, as well as a compromise over the water rights. Chaffey had determined that

ABOVE: Richard Gird came to California in 1881 from Tombstone, Arizona. He purchased a 640-acre ranch from Joseph Bridger, and gradually increased his holdings to nearly 50,000 acres. In 1887 he decided to sell 23,000 acres in 10-acre lots, creating a townsite with the name Chino. Courtesy, Dorothy Grier, Chino Historical Society

LEFT: Flumes or sluices, like this one in Stoddard Canyon, carried water from the mountains to the new settlements on the plains. Courtesy, Ontario City Library, Model Colony History Room

ABOVE: *This view of Euclid Avenue, taken around 1890 from a specially erected tower, shows the Ontario Hotel on the left and the Southern Pacific Hotel on the right. The three-story building in the distance is Chaffey College. Courtesy, Ontario City Library, Model Colony History Room*

RIGHT: *The San Antonio Light and Power Company cut this tunnel through Hogsback in 1892. The tunnel brought water to the power plant located at the foot of Hogsback Grade on San Antonio Creek. Courtesy, Ontario City Library, Model Colony History Room*

the most important water supply lay not in the run-off waters, but underground in the deep gravels of the alluvium. He was more than willing to concede half the rights to Pomona.

Garcia accepted the Chaffey offer, and they traveled to San Francisco to complete the arrangements which included letting Pomona have half the water rights for the surface water in San Antonio Canyon. On September 18, 1882, the Chaffeys purchased 6,216 acres of the Cucamonga Rancho for the sum of $60,000.

Water rights, however, weren't enough to make the Ontario colony a going concern. Railroad facilities were crucial, and the Southern Pacific Railroad tracks went through land to the south of the Cucamonga Rancho purchase—land that was owned by Mills, Wicks, and John A. Benson. For $20,030.80, George Chaffey acquired 2,500 acres between the Ontario townsite and Rancho Cucamonga. He had brought his colony land to the Southern Pacific Railroad, and in the process acquired more water rights.

In addition, Chaffey bid on the 114-acre M.M. Kincaid Rancho from S.H. Ferris of Riverside. The land had been granted to Kincaid in 1865 by U.S. patent, and his descendants had set out grapevines and a peach orchard. Again Wicks and Mills competed for San Antonio land and the valuable water rights. And again George Chaffey outmaneuvered them, and purchased the land for $11,000. By the end of September 1882 he had all the land and water rights for the new colony. All that was left was to plan and plat the colony.

Reminiscing in 1925 to Claremont resident Charles J. Booth, George Chaffey said he conceived his plan for laying out Ontario in the shade of M.M. Kincaid's old peach trees near the mouth of San Antonio Canyon. "That is where I went to plan this scheme. I laid out there all day long and after a time I had it pretty well in mind. I got my surveyor and the thing was under way," Chaffey said. The surveyor, of course, was J.C. Dunlap.

George Chaffey's plan for Ontario embodied four basic concepts that were later formalized in all land sale contracts:

1. Distribute the water over the whole tract to each farm lot in cement pipes, each holder to share in the water proportionately to his holding irrespective of distance from the source;

2. Construct a main thoroughfare from one end of the settlement to the other, and lay it out in such a way that it will be a thing of beauty forever;

3. Provide a College for the agricultural education of the people of the colony and for the general education of their children;

4. Secure the best possible class of settlers by a reversionary clause in the deeds to each allotment forbidding absolutely the sale of intoxicating liquor.

The Layout

Intending to attract as many Canadians as possible, Chaffey named his colony for his home Canadian province. To pay some kind of homage to the engineering and mathematical expertise responsible for the planning of the colony, he named the main boulevard, which ran more than seven miles from its southernmost boundaries to the mountains, for Euclid, the ancient Greek geometrician. Eventually Euclid Avenue was extended to 15 miles in length.

Ontario was laid out on paper before it was surveyed. Euclid Avenue was to be a 200-foot-wide double drive, most likely modeled after the much acclaimed and very beautiful Magnolia Avenue in Riverside. Euclid's center parkway was to be flanked by a 65-foot-wide drive on each side. Every half-mile, paralleling Euclid to the east and west, were 65-foot-wide avenues. North and south, at quarter-mile

ELEVATION
1000-2500 FT.
POPULATION 4500

ONTARIO

ELECTRIC CARS
TO MOUNTAINS
7 MILES.

These five young ladies posed in front of the Frankish fountain in about 1907. The sign welcomes train passengers passing through Ontario. Courtesy, Ontario City Library, Model Colony History Room

We went inside and found George Chaffey there. We at once thought: What a clear-sighted, handsome, well set-up man this is. He just personified that quality of determination and practical mindedness and enterprise that could not help but impress anybody, and that feeling was heightened by the cordiality with which he received us . . . he helped us in a thousand ways to get an understanding of what the problems were. He told us that if we wished to see what was regarded as a model irrigation settlement we should stop off at Ontario on our way East, where his brother and he had established a settlement in its initial stages . . . Accordingly, Messrs. Deakin, Dow and myself went to Ontario, and there we met W.B. Chaffey, a man of quite a different type physically. George had a square full black beard and was a well set-up man. W.B. was of spare build—but one who had all the appearance of being full of purpose and determination.

Deakin's straightforward interest in irrigation, coupled with the challenge of watering the deserts of Victoria and the prospect of the huge land grants the Australian government was all but giving away to squatters, was an irresistable lure to the two young Canadians. Toward the end of 1885 the Chaffeys sent a representative to Australia to open negotiations with Deakin. Their delegate, Stephen H. Cureton, had previously spent time in Australia, and George had met him in Bakersfield during one of his many trips to an antimony mine he was interested in.

Cureton's misleadingly optimistic report to the Chaffeys, promising unlimited land and possibly a cash bonus for their irrigation expertise, induced George to make a trip to Australia. Intent on negotiating an irrigation colony with Alfred Deakin, Chaffey sailed for Sydney from Los Angeles on January 11, 1886. A few weeks later he cabled William to sell their interests in Ontario.

Instead of the great profits George Chaffey expected from the judicious sale of Ontario lands and holdings, says Alexander in his *Life of George Chaffey*, "W.B. sold out lock, stock and barrel to the Ontario Land and Improvement Company . . ."

According to Bernice Bedford Conley's *Dreamers and Dwellers*, on March 3, 1886, the new land company received through a deed of trust

. . . 7,500 acres of land, the Ontario Hotel, the water works, and San Antonio Water Company interests, land in San Antonio Canyon covering the development of water, and even the horses, implements, office and office fixtures, and all other personal property belong(ing) to George and William Chaffey and the other original trustees.

The amount W.B. realized from the sale, $275,000, was a mere $25,000 more than the amount the Chaffeys had invested in Ontario. As Alexander notes, "The Chaffeys thus sacrificed everything to come to Australia . . ."

In Australia, the brothers founded the two irrigation colonies of Mildura and Renmark in the region of Victoria. For the Chaffeys, the result of their work was financially disappointing and at one point they were all but impoverished. William, however, stayed in Mildura to make good his promises to the town. He became one of Mildura's most respected citizens, and eventually the citizens erected a statue in his memory.

George returned undaunted to the United States in 1897, sadder but wiser. After several disappointing ventures in other parts of the country, he returned to California, where he helped a rapidly growing Ontario with a water shortage, and then proceeded to irrigate the Imperial Valley.

The Ontario Land and Improvement Company

Upon learning that the Chaffeys wanted to sell out, Charles Frankish, a Riverside

Charles Frankish came to Ontario in March 1886 as a member and resident manager of the Ontario Land and Improvement Company. He was responsible for much of the development south of A Street and remained a dominant force in Ontario well into the twentieth century. Courtesy, Ontario City Library, Model Colony History Room

orange grove owner, quickly formed the Ontario Land and Improvement Company, which went on to realize the profits originally envisioned by George Chaffey. Five of the 10 original members of the new company signed the agreement papers, including Charles Frankish of Riverside; Hugh Livingston Macneil of Los Angeles; Dan McFarland of Los Angeles; Oliver Sheppard Picher of Pasadena; and Lyman Stewart of Los Angeles.

The other early trustees were Frederick J. Gissing of Toronto; George C. Hagar of Orange; Charles Edward Harwood of Springfield, Missouri; Godfrey T. Stamm of Los Angeles; and Milton Stewart of Titusville, Pennsylvania. Later, Samuel Prescott Hildreth, of Wheeling, West Virginia, and Alfred Perez Harwood, Charles Harwood's brother, bought into the company.

Charles Frankish moved from Riverside to become the Model Colony's manager and resident agent. Ultimately, he had as great a hand in Ontario's development as did the Chaffeys.

Land Boom and the Railroads

The Ontario Land and Improvement Company comprised for the most part real estate speculators, who made their Ontario purchase at the cutting edge of the Great California Land Boom. The boom lasted nearly two years, roughly from the end of 1886 to the first part of 1888. A preposterous rate war between the Southern Pacific and Santa Fe railroads is generally credited as the cause of the boom.

From the beginning, the Ontario developers understood that the colony's success was dependent upon the railroad lines, which in California were controlled by the Big Four—Leland Stanford, Charles Crocker, Collis P. Huntington, and Mark Hopkins. The railroad all but held cities' futures for ransom, requiring them to pay in cash and land for the privilege of having local spurs and depots. Since the coast-to-coast link-up in Utah in 1869,

the Central Pacific had dominated the northern part of the state and there was no railroad in Southern California. The Big Four, in order to maintain their California monopoly, formed the Southern Pacific Railroad in December of 1865. They were authorized to lay track along the coast and to receive subsidies from those counties south of Santa Clara.

Los Angeles county surrendered the fledgling Los Angeles and San Pedro Railroad plus $600,000 and paid for the construction of a major depot. Since the agreement was drawn up by Rancho San Jose's Francisco Palomares, the future site of Pomona was ensured access to the Southern Pacific. In 1873 track reached Spadra, and by 1875 a station was established east of Spadra at the site of the future town of Pomona.

While the line passed through the Ontario colony site, it did not stop. In the early days of the colony's development, George Chaffey would have visitors take the train to Cucamonga; he drove there with a carriage to collect visitors and potential buyers and took them on a tour of Etiwanda and Ontario. Prior to completion of the $10,000 Ontario Hotel in May of 1883, guests would stay at the Etiwanda home Chaffey had purchased from Captain Garcia.

In anticipation of regular train stops, George Chaffey built his new hotel and a depot across the street from each other at the foot of Euclid near the Southern Pacific tracks. In January 1883 the *Ontario Fruit Grower* announced that trains were to make regular stops in Ontario. To further advertise Ontario and counter rumors spread by Pomona real estate interests that there was no water in the new colony, Chaffey installed a fountain at the corner of Euclid Avenue and the Southern Pacific tracks. Each time a train passed through, the fountain was turned on to tout Ontario's abundant water supply.

With the completion of the depot and the hotel, the world had access to Ontario.

The Hotpoint Electric Company, part of General Electric, was one of Ontario's biggest employers. Staff members had their own social club and enjoyed a variety of activities. The Hotpoint Baseball Team, shown here, was the Ontario Night League champion in 1933. Courtesy, Ontario City Library, Model Colony History Room

Into the Twentieth Century

Railroad rate wars began with the breaking of the Southern Pacific monopoly, signaled by the 1882 completion of a second rail line through Southern California from San Diego to Colton. The California Southern Railroad was backed by San Diego businessmen in partnership with another business group from nearby National City, in full cooperation with the Santa Fe. When the California Southern Railroad finally linked up with the Santa Fe at Cajon Pass above San Bernardino in 1885, giving the country two competing transcontinental railroads, the land boom was on.

Passenger rates from the East Coast to Los Angeles were around $125 in 1883. By the time the Santa Fe drove its Golden Spike at Cajon Pass they were down to $95. But even $95 was beyond the reach of most people, as farm workers generally earned between $400 and $600 a year.

The rate war climaxed on March 6, 1887. In the morning, the Southern Pacific and Santa Fe rates matched at $12. Santa Fe then dropped to $10, followed by the Southern Pacific. The Santa Fe cut again to $8, and was matched. In the heat of the moment the Southern Pacific began to beat its own rates, cutting them to $6, then to $4. Shortly after noon, the Southern Pacific announced a rate of $1, although no tickets for that amount were sold. Soon the furor died down and the rates went up, but not so much that they kept people away. In 1887 more than 120,000 people were transported to Los Angeles by the Southern Pacific alone. The Santa Fe was bringing in three and four passenger trains a day, and many of these newcomers made their way to Ontario.

Chaffey College of Agriculture

Along with plans for the depot and the hotel, the Chaffeys developed plans for the Chaffey College of Agriculture. George Chaffey believed that by endowing an institution of higher learning, he would be able to attract quality settlers—specifically families.

A 20-acre site at the corner of Euclid Avenue and Fourth Street was set aside for the new college. Chaffey arranged for the University of Southern California (USC) to supervise the trust fund he established, as well as develop the college's building plans. Six members of the USC board of trustees were named to the Chaffey College board. The deed of trust was signed on December 22, 1882.

Although Ontario was virtually uninhabited when the cornerstone was laid during a huge celebration on March 17, 1883, the party and banquet, a cleverly orchestrated media event, was attended by 500 people.

George Chaffey brought in two trainloads of prospective buyers, and newspaper reporters from as far away as San Francisco arrived. Wheeled conveyances of all sorts met the party-goers at the tracks and hauled them the seven-and-one-half miles up the specially graded, but as yet unplanted, Euclid Avenue to the mesa at the foot of the mountains where the view is as spectacular as any in Southern California.

After a bountiful lunch and a few flowery speeches, the group was hauled back down Euclid, creating a seven-mile-long

The 1890 class was the first to graduate from the new Chaffey College. The class consisted of only three students; S.J. Holmes (not pictured), Helen Dyer (right), and Alma Wilmot (left). The graduation stage featured an ivy arch with the school's motto "possunt quia posse videntur" spelled out in evergreen. A loose translation of the motto is "they can do it because they think they can do it." Courtesy, Ontario City Library, Model Colony History Room

procession to the college site, where the foundations were already laid and the cornerstone ready to be placed. They were addressed by Judge R.M. Widney, chairman of the board of directors of USC, E.F. Spence, another USC board member, and USC president the Reverend M.M. Bovard.

By the end of the day, which saw visitors chasing jack rabbits and kicking through the sagebrush for the stakes marking the school property, Ontario had a college as well as a large number of new residents.

When completed, the college had 15 classrooms, a chapel, a library, and two dormitories, for a total cost of $17,000. The school operated as a private boarding school and in 1885 boasted 15 students and a faculty of three. Curriculum consisted primarily of high school courses and drew students from such areas as Riverside and Hemet, where there were, as yet, no public schools. School catalogues emphasized

the moral atmosphere of the college, stating that combined with the excellent morals of the town of Ontario, Chaffey was "able to offer city advantages without city dangers." Students were required to attend the daily devotionals in the chapel and were encouraged to attend the church of their choice.

The completion of the college marked the beginning of the colony's rapid growth into both an agricultural settlement and a small city. Tree planting symbolized both efforts.

Crops and Plantings

The trees along Euclid Avenue were the first in the new colony and the first to benefit from the elaborate irrigation system. Swiss emigrant E.J. Jaquet directed the Euclid Avenue plantings of pepper trees, palms, eucalyptus, and grevillea, which made the boulevard into one of the most attractive in the world. The trees were planted in four rows along the 200-foot-wide boulevard. The center divider, which has an average width of 65 feet, was planted with more than 2,000 pepper trees. The eucalyptus and grevillea lined the outer edges of the street. More than 5,000 trees were planted in all.

Isaac Whittaker, the man who built the first house in Ontario, also planted the first orange tree. The first citrus orchards, however, were started by George and William's brother, Dr. Elswood Chaffey, also the colony's first doctor. (Elswood Chaffey's son Heber Elswood, born on April 17, 1884, was Ontario's first baby.) Had it not been for the Ontario colony's close Riverside connections and Riverside's experiments with citriculture, it is possible that citrus orchards in Ontario would not have appeared until a much later date. Ontario took an active role in the development of what Harry Lawton and Lewis G. Weathers, in their monograph "The Origins of Citrus Research in California," call "the stumbling beginnings of California's citrus industry."

According to a note in *Ontario: From A to Z*, the *Los Angeles Times* reported on May 6, 1885, that "Fred L. Alles of this city has grown on his place at Ontario the first orange produced in that settlement. A plaster cast is to be made of it." By 1889, 410 acres had been developed for citrus. Olive and deciduous fruit groves also made their appearance during this period. While citrus and grapes would become Ontario's principal crops, in the early years of agricultural development deciduous fruits—primarily peaches and apricots—played a large part in the area's economy.

The Settlement

Ontario's first family put up their tent on January 11, 1883, on a lot that Isaac W. Whittaker had purchased on December 27, 1882. Whittaker recalled their pioneering adventure for the *Ontario Daily Republican* in 1911. The paper's account states:

. . . accompanied by wife, started out from Los Angeles on January 11, and drove to Pomona, where they put up for the night.

The next morning they drove over through the sagebrush to Ontario. While the streets were staked out, the stakes could not be seen for the brush and Mr. Whittaker was up against it when it came to finding his ten acres. After trying for some time in vain to locate his place, he started out to find the Chaffeys and finally located William Chaffey.

It was no easy matter for Chaffey to find the place, but after counting up the streets and pacing off the lots he finally managed to locate the Whittaker property, and it was here that the first domicile, in the shape of a tent, was erected in the new city of Ontario.

In this tent Mr. Whittaker lived with his wife for about a month, at the end of which time he was able to get lumber and build a small house.

Within the year the Whittakers had more than 50 neighbors scattered throughout the colony. By October 1885 a school district had been formed, the library was in the planning stage, A.E. Payne's grocery store was up for sale, the post office was established, and there was a general store owned by D.T. Jones and a livery stable owned by Moores and Smith. A telegraph office appeared in December, and on December 11 the first telegraph message was sent from Ontario.

In October 1885 Ernest P. Clarke made his initial foray into the colony to find out if it was ready for a weekly newspaper. A name was picked and on December 16, 1885, the *Ontario Record* made its debut. That year saw the organization of two church congregations, the Methodist and the Congregational, as well as the opening of the Chaffey College of Agriculture. The colony had its first drug store, thanks to Dr. E.D. Watson. Other commercial enterprises included a shoe store located inside Drew's furniture store, a poultry yard, and a meat market.

The first baby born in the new colony was Heber Elswood Chaffey, born on April 17, 1884. Courtesy, Ontario City Library, Model Colony History Room

ABOVE: *The first telegraph message to be transmitted from Ontario was sent on December 11, 1885. North Ontario's postal telegraph office, shown here, was located in a private home so the operator could always be near her work. Courtesy, Ontario City Library, Model Colony History Room*

RIGHT: *The first house in Ontario was built by Isaac W. Whittaker. He purchased a 10-acre parcel on Fifth Street west of Euclid Avenue where he built this two-story wooden home and planted orange trees. During construction of the home, he and his wife lived in a tent on the site. Courtesy, Ontario City Library, Model Colony History Room*

Ontario suffered several setbacks, not the least of which were due to the area's climatic vagaries. In 1887 many of the colony's buildings and most of its groves were devastated by violent Santa Ana winds. In the recovery process, residents learned new pruning methods, began to plant rows of tall trees to act as wind breaks, and used much sturdier building methods in erecting their structures.

In many respects, the year 1887 marked the end of the colonial period for Ontario. In less than five years it had become a bustling town with a well-organized citizenry and was on its way to becoming a self-contained political unit. Certainly Ontarians had wasted no time in developing all the economic and social bases residents could ask for. Churches played a prominent part in the colony, and the Methodist and Presbyterian churches were preparing to build; social clubs were established and met regularly in homes and sometimes at the hotel; one commercial block had been completed and another was on its way. The *Ontario Record* prospered after a shaky beginning and was relocated to a new brick building of its own.

Water, though, was increasingly a problem. The system was failing to meet the settlement's needs, and several years of drought paved the way for Ontario's incorporation as a town over the protests of the Ontario Land Company, which had bought out the Chaffeys and was responsible for so much of the colony's prosperity and growth.

On March 13, 1887, the Ontario Land Company, which until then had no power to buy new land, only the ability to sell off the original purchase, decided to incorporate to protect its investment, and the investors filed articles of incorporation with Sacramento. The new corporation had the power to buy and sell land and water, make improvements, and control the supply and distribution of water.

That same year citizens started clamoring for incorporation of Ontario as a town.

A committee led by Dr. Edmund Bedford of North Ontario and Ernest P. Clarke, the *Record*'s owner, urged for incorporation of the colony for the purpose of having greater local control and a more equitable tax base.

It was not to the advantage of the land company to have the colony incorporate. Arguments for and against raged for months on the street corners and in the newspaper. In March 1888 the Board of Supervisors ordered an election for April 16. Incorporation of Ontario was defeated at the polls, 128 to 55.

Ironically, failure of the colony's famous water system to deliver during drought conditions led to a successful incorporation movement in 1891. The section hardest hit by the water problem was the increasingly populous half-mile-square townsite bordered by the Southern Pacific Railroad tracks to the south, G Street to the north, Sultana Avenue to the east, and Vine Avenue to the west, with Euclid Avenue at its center.

On August 14, 1891, during a mass meeting held at Sweet's Hall, citizens appointed a committee to meet with the San Antonio Water Company. Together, the committee and the water company proposed to issue bonds to raise the money to improve the system. Water stock was already held in trust for the town, but it could not be used as collateral to raise the money to improve the water delivery system.

Judge R.M. Widney determined the stock could be transferred only to the water company, a corporation, or an individual. He advised that with incorporation, the stock could be turned over to the town, which could in turn borrow on the stock or issue bonds.

After several months of canvassing citizens, and numerous newspaper articles outlining the pros and cons, an election was held on November 21, 1891. The result was 40 votes for incorporation and 31 against. On December 8 the San

ABOVE: The Park Hotel, located on West C Street between Euclid and Laurel avenues was just one of a number of hotels in the downtown area at the turn of the century. In 1909 meals were only 25 cents while room rates ranged from 25 to 50 cents. Courtesy, Ontario City Library, Model Colony History Room

RIGHT: Ontario's first school was established in 1884 and held classes in the attic of a carpenter's shop. Central School, pictured, was completed in January 1887 at a cost of $6,000. It accommodated 250 pupils. Courtesy, Ontario City Library, Model Colony History Room

Bernardino County Board of Supervisors declared the half-mile-square area to be a municipality of the sixth class. Certification was filed with the secretary of state on December 10. The first board of trustees was composed of A.E. Tracy, David T. Jones, David S. Cochran, John P. Ensley, and William T. Randall. E. Dubois was clerk, John P. Robertson was treasurer, and L.J.E. Tyler was marshal.

Spurred by rumors that North Ontario was about to incorporate as far south as G Street, in May 1901 the city expanded its limits from the original half-mile-square townsite to 10 square miles, making the population jump from 722 to 4,274. The expansion included virtually all of the original colony lands up to San Antonio Heights. The exception was a small area occupied by North Ontario's business district. The colony was growing rapidly, holding its own in the twentieth century.

Eleanor Freeman described 1904 Ontario in her article in Ingersoll's *Century Annals of San Bernardino County 1769-1904*:

. . . the plains of the Ontario and Cucamonga settlements are a garden-spot of the earth. Near the center of the Ontario colony lies the town, the spires of its churches, the belfries of its school houses and the brick buildings of its business streets standing out against the greenness of the trees that embower the place. Wide avenues lead out from the town through the surrounding colony and an electric line, with convenient and comfortable cars, carries one from the southern limit of the settlement to the foothills at the mouth of the San Antonio canyon—nearly seven miles . . .

Here the orange and the lemon, the olive and the grape, flowers of every variety, gardens and fields are all in the perfection of growth and of yield. One looks in vain for the haunts of vice and poverty in this vicinity. The fertile soil rewards its tiller so generously that the humblest home shelters comfort and what—in less favored localities—would be luxury.

The newcomer can hardly be persuaded

that all this luxuriance of vegetation, that the thriving town with its lines of steel rails extending far to the east and the west, with its delightful homes, its commodious school houses, its numerous churches and its handsome business blocks is all the result of less than twenty-two years of occupation.

Modern Conveniences

In the early years of its founding, Ontario acquired much of the technology and many of the modern conveniences generally attributed to the widespread use of electricity.

By 1882 the Chaffeys had installed the first long-distance telephone line in the world. The line connected the towns of Etiwanda, Riverside, San Bernardino, Colton, Redlands, and Lugonia. The Etiwanda line was owned by the Chaffeys, while the Redlands line was owned by two other entrepreneurs, and a Los Angeles company owned the San Bernardino system. In 1883, through negotiations with the Los Angeles company, the Chaffeys acquired a phone line that connected George Chaffey's house in Etiwanda to Ontario as well as Los Angeles.

By the early 1890s a general service was established at one of Ontario's three stores, and in 1907 the San Bernardino Valley Telephone and Telegraph Company opened an office at 112 West A Street. There were 130 subscribers.

George Chaffey installed the first electric light in Southern California at his Etiwanda home in 1882. To power it he built the first hydroelectric dynamo in the western United States. Ironically, Chaffey was to make Los Angeles—whose city fathers did not want a small upstart colony to outshine them—the first city in the United States to be lighted exclusively by electricity.

Powered by an electrical generating apparatus developed by Chaffey, the first electric lights in Ontario lit the Workman's Lodge banquet and installation on January 4, 1886. The generator was kept in storage

After Ontario's incorporation on December 10, 1891, David T. Jones was elected president of the newly formed Board of Trustees, forerunners of the mayor and city council. Courtesy, Ontario City Library, Model Colony History Room

for use on special occasions, and Ontario did not receive full electric service until 1895.

The Ontario Electric Company was organized on February 16, 1895, for the purpose of operating the electric railway up Euclid Avenue's median, and to generate and sell electricity. Ontario's powerhouse was completed in the summer of 1895. In the fall, the rest of the equipment to light the streets was in place. For Christmas, an arc light in the yard of the Ontario Hotel illuminated the festivities.

By 1909 the company had 1,300 subscribers. In 1928 the service was sold to Southern California Edison, and by 1935 there were more than 10,000 subscribers served in Ontario, Upland, Alta Loma, Cucamonga, Camp Baldy, Narod, Norco, and La Sierra.

Chaffey's colony plans had also called for building an electric rail through the middle of the settlement, using the area at the center of Euclid Avenue. The first track was laid in 1888 under the aegis of the Ontario Land and Improvement Company. Charles Frankish was instrumental in forming the Ontario and San Antonio Heights Railway Company, with C.C. Harwood as president. It was Harwood who acquired the first cars from a St. Louis company, and on December 8, 1888, the *Observer* noted that the "streetcars arrived yesterday and they are daisies."

The line went into operation on December 10, 1888, but until electricity was available, horses and mules provided the power for getting up the 2 percent grade and gravity provided the return power. James B. Tays is credited with developing the remarkable and soon-famous system that had the mules hop on board and get a labor-free seven-mile ride down the grade. Local legend has it that when one of the mules was sold to a farmer, the mule pulled the plow rapidly up the first furrow, but when it reached the end it stopped and wanted a ride back.

During the maiden trip after electrification on December 14, 1895, the brakes on the car failed to take hold. With bonnet ribbons flying, the riders, mostly members of the Frankish family, got a three-mile downhill thrill-ride before things were brought under control.

It shouldn't be surprising, then, that Ontario's first modern industry also had to do with putting the power of electricity to work—in an iron that distributed heat evenly, clear to the point. The developer of the internationally famous Hotpoint iron was Earl Holmes Richardson, an employee of the Ontario Electric Company.

Richardson came to Pomona looking for a job after 5 years with an Aurora, Illinois, electric company, where he had been a lineman and a motor repairman, and had also gained experience doing armature wiring.

Shortly after Richardson came to the area, Ontario's new electric plant burst a water pipe. A portion of the stone wall was torn out by the rushing water and wet mortar, and rocks and dirt wrecked the generator. Charles Frankish hired Richardson to repair the generator, and eventually he took charge of the San Antonio Heights powerhouse, living with his wife and daughter in a couple of tents next to the edifice known as the Stone Castle.

Experimenting with appliances to make life more comfortable for his family, Richardson first developed an electric room heater, then a cooking stove. These he sold to Ontario residents. At the same time he was experimenting with appliances and the resistance coil, the electric company found it was producing far more electricity than local residents could use for their lighting and irrigation pumps. The company was eager to find more uses for its product.

Richardson, after much trial and

error, produced an electric iron that was heated by a single coil. He took it to the company's board, which helped him market the product. In 1906 Richardson severed connections with the local power company and set up shop as the Pacific Electric Heating Company with a partner, B.C. Shephard, a former secretary in the power company.

Initially, their product was well received, but then complaints began to come in. It didn't get hot enough at the point, and the uneven temperature on the bottom caused the starch to stick and the clothing to burn. He solved the problem by bringing together two resistor elements in a "V" shape at the tip of the iron. Hence the name for his new iron, "Hotpoint."

The company struggled financially, Shephard gave up, and just before reaching total financial ruin, Richardson found a backer in Willis Booth, a Los Angeles businessman. In 1906 the company moved to Lemon and Main. By 1932 the plant was producing 1,500 irons a day, more than they put out in an entire year in the early days.

In 1933 the plant became a unit of the General Electric Company, providing the local economy with an annual payroll of more than $500,000.

Besides eagerly embracing modern public transportation in the form of the electric car line on Euclid Avenue, Ontarians wasted no time in introducing the auto-

Earl H. Richardson, inventor of the Hotpoint iron, gained much of his electrical knowledge by working as a motor repairman on electric streetcars in Aurora, Illinois. Within 10 years of his coming to Pomona he started the Pacific Electric Heating Company. In addition to managing his company, Richardson devoted much of his time to the city council and Chamber of Commerce. Courtesy, Ontario City Library, Model Colony History Room

While operating the "Stone Castle" powerhouse in San Antonio Heights, E.H. Richardson found himself with spare time and spare electricity. After experimenting with various household appliances, he developed the electric iron. This is the first Hotpoint iron manufactured by his Pacific Heating Company. Courtesy, Ontario City Library, Model Colony History Room

ABOVE: The gravity mule car was Ontario's first public transportation system, operating from late 1888 to 1895. Mules or horses pulled the car up Euclid Avenue to San Antonio Heights and made the seven-mile return trip on a platform at the rear of the car. Courtesy, Ontario City Library, Model Colony History Room

RIGHT: Ontario's mule-powered streetcar system was electrified in 1895 with power supplied by a plant in San Antonio Heights. The system became part of the Pacific Electric Line in 1912. Courtesy, Ontario City Library, Model Colony History Room

mobile into the social and work world. By 1910 the gasoline-powered vehicles were so entrenched in American life that they were beginning to replace horse-drawn transportation on a large scale.

The Ontario fire department acquired its first fire truck from Ontario farm equipment dealer F.A.C. Drew, Sr. It was a white six-cylinder Mitchell touring car with a truck body fitted on to it.

The first "horseless carriage" sold in San Bernardino County had an Ontario connection. The 1902 Cadillac with engine No. 13 was purchased by George D. Haven, great-uncle of Webster H. Thomas, the owner of the Thomas Winery. The nine-horsepower, one-cylinder engine could achieve a top speed of 18 miles per hour on the straightaway. The red car had neither top nor windshield, and was right-hand drive.

By 1910 Ontario was supporting the Ocean-to-Ocean highway effort. The proposed route from Los Angeles to New York City was to pass through Ontario. Auto sales agents, garages, and gas stations sprang up everywhere, and by May 1911 more than 32 makes of automobiles could be spotted on Ontario's streets. According to Conley's *Dreamers and Dwellers*, "there was one car for every 24 citizens, about 175 cars valued at $250,000."

Banking and Newspapers

Ontario's first bank has operated continuously for more than a century, since it was established in 1887 by Godfrey Stamm as the Ontario State Bank. In 1902 it was taken over by George and Andrew Chaffey, becoming the First National Bank of Ontario and operating as such until 1963, when it became the First National Bank and Trust Company. In 1979 the bank converted to state charter and became First Trust Bank.

A second bank, Citizens Bank, opened on April 7, 1890, with J.P. Robertson as president and M.V. McQuigg as cashier. That bank occupied several locations over the

years, opening first in the Brooks Block in the Southern Pacific Hotel building. In 1911 it consolidated with the First National Bank of Ontario.

Ontario National Bank was formed on February 22, 1911, by several prominent citizens: George McCrea, E. Joseph Sandford, B. Campbell, J.B. Draper, J.S. Armstrong, Homer Berger, George C. Freeman, and Judge J.R. Pollock. This bank also went through several transformations. It was purchased by the Liberty Bank of America in 1927, which merged with the Bank of Italy in 1928, which was in turn purchased by the Bank of America.

While Ontario's banks have been extremely influential over the years, another institution has been just as important in setting the tone of Ontario's development—newspapers. Since Ontario's founding, the community's newspapers have alway played an important role in influencing public opinion.

The colony's first newspaper, the *Ontario Fruit Grower*, was published by L.M. Holt from December 4, 1882, until May 1884. The colony was then without a paper until December 1885, when Ernest P. Clarke began publishing the *Ontario Record*.

The *Record* became one of California's most enduring weeklies and did not shut down until 1963. That left the *Chino Champion*, founded in 1887, with the honor of being the oldest continuously published weekly newspaper in California, still publishing in 1989.

In 1910 F.E. Unholz, owner and editor of the *Record* since 1906, took a chance that the community was ready for a daily. On September 12, 1910, he published the first edition of the *Daily Republican*. A year later Unholz sold his interests in both the weekly and the daily to Crombie Allen and H.L. Allen, and the *Republican* was renamed the *Daily Report*. The Allens published both papers until 1930, when Jerene and Frank B. Appleby bought them out. Frank Appleby died in 1936, and his wife

E.P. Clarke, editor and co-owner of the Ontario Record *newspaper, came to Ontario in 1885. The first issue of the weekly newspaper was published on December 13, 1885. Clarke and his newspaper editorials were instrumental in rallying support for Ontario's incorporation prior to the November 1891 election. Courtesy, Ontario City Library, Model Colony History Room*

took over the operation.

More than any previous publisher, Jerene Appleby Harnish used the paper's editorial influence to affect the town's directions, not hesitating to take controversial stances on issues. J. Frederic Blitstein, in his 1971 doctoral thesis "America's Turmoil: A View From the Suburbs," stated that while the *Daily Report* still wielded community influence it "no way compares to the times when Mrs. J. Harnish ruled with the conservative power of hell and fire. Her word was law as she dictated council policy."

Over the years several other weeklies have come and gone. Early in the colony's history, in April 1887, the *Observer* came on the scene, only to merge with the *Record* in 1901. And in 1918 D.D. McDonald founded the Ontario *Herald* and the *Outlook*, which published through the early 1950s.

In 1933 Ignacio Lopez began publishing a Spanish-language newspaper, *El Espectador*. That paper ceased being printed in 1960.

Ontario Goes to War

One of the most decisive events in the twentieth century was the advent of the war in Europe on July 28, 1914. Even though automation, mass production, automobiles, and heavier-than-air flying machines were gradually making their way into the lives of citizens, the need for war machinery was the overwhelming factor that forced social, communication, and technological change.

Ontario, like other cities across the nation, joined President Woodrow Wilson in his quest to maintain neutrality in the war that was devastating Europe. While Wilson stubbornly stuck to the policy of neutrality, American citizens began to doubt that the United States could stay out of the war. In 1914 Ontario residents, demonstrating evidence of sympathy for the war effort against the Germans, formed the British Relief Society to enlist aid for the "widows, orphans and others left behind when their

bread-winners were away fighting . . ." Public sentiment increasingly swung away from neutrality with each new report of a German atrocity. In 1917 Congress, unable to maintain neutrality any longer, declared war on Germany. More than 1,500 men from the West End, including Ontario, were registered for the draft.

Ontario jumped into the war effort wholeheartedly. Residents sold and bought Liberty Bonds. J. Stitt Wilson roused the populace with a series of patriotic addresses. Isaac Jones headed the Red Cross drive, which topped the $10,000 goal by several thousand dollars. Women knitted warm clothing for the soldiers, and for the first time in history left the home in large numbers to work in the factories. In Ontario these were primarily the fruit packinghouses.

Eventually, 1,540 men from the Ontario area were registered for the draft. Homer "Curley" Runyon became the first Ontario man to get called up. On February 19, 1918, local man Ralph T. Kingery became the first Californian to be killed in action in France. Before the end of the war, 19 Ontario men died overseas.

Returned servicemen met on August 4, 1919, to organize a group that eventually became a chapter of the national American Legion. Archie D. Mitchell was elected president of the group and G.R. Jenkins was chosen to be secretary.

Airport of the Future

During the war aviation became firmly established, losing its "novelty" status. Air Corps veterans and flight-smitten young men began building flying machines and barnstorming the countryside, showing off and giving rides to the public. It wasn't long before commercial benefits became apparent. Mail-carrying air routes made their appearance, shortly followed by fledgling airlines for passenger travel.

Ontario, again a leader in modern developments, became the second California

LEFT: Publisher of the Ontario Daily Report from 1912 to 1930, Crombie Allen called himself "the oldest printer's devil in Ontario." He published the first issue of the paper on January 1, 1912. Allen was a member of the California Legislature and was active in the California Press Association. In 1985 that organization elected him to the California Newspaper Hall of Fame. Courtesy, Ontario City Library, Model Colony History Room

ABOVE: Charles Frankish—accompanied by his son Hugh, wife Eliza, and friends—sits at the wheel of his "Old Northern" automobile near his Emporia Street home in 1909. Courtesy, Ontario City Library, Model Colony History Room

Ontario's Fire Department was organized by the city's Board of Trustees in 1905 with W.M. Hart as its chief. A new fire station was built in 1907 on the east side of Euclid Avenue between C and D streets. Until that time the volunteer department worked out of the Masonic Hall. Courtesy, Ontario City Library, Model Colony History Room

city to establish a municipal airport. In 1923, at the instigation of World War I veteran and Ontario city attorney Archie Delwood Mitchell, a group of flyers, including Waldo D. Waterman, Hugh H. Wolfe, Allan Couch, H.B. Banta, C.C. Minton, and C.E.T. Smith formed the Ontario Aircraft Corporation. Their airfield was a dirt strip named Latimer Field for the orange packing company next door. It was located just west of San Antonio Avenue between the Southern Pacific and Union Pacific tracks. Their first aircraft was a Curtiss JN 4 "Jenny." Waterman was instructor and mechanic. In 1924 the corporation acquired and modified for land use four Boeing flying boats and established the ill-fated Big Bear Airline. It was an unsuccessful venture, marred from the beginning by a crash landing in Big Bear Lake.

On December 29, 1929, the city purchased 30 acres as an airport site off California Street between the Southern Pacific and Union Pacific tracks, nearly two miles east of Euclid—far from downtown development, but in an excellent position to take advantage of nearby rail shipping. The airport's growth remained static through the Depression; air traffic was accommodated with a single dirt strip and hangar.

Undoubtedly, the presence of the airport and the growth of the aeronautics industry led to the introduction of the aeronautics vocational program at Chaffey College in 1934. It was the first large-scale vocational program other than agriculture and commerce to be added to the curriculum. Courses offered over the years included Theory of Flight, The Airplane Engine and Airplane Construction, Meteorology, Avigation (aerial navigation), Fundamentals of Aeronautical Engineering, Engine Repair and Maintenance, and Airplane Drafting.

Almost without hesitation Ontario slipped into the technological twentieth century and became, in spite of its relatively small population, a flourishing modern city. It was graced with its world-famous avenue, which was lined with businesses and banks

The Ontario Aircraft Corporation was formed in 1923 with Waldo D. Waterman as manager. Waterman was the most experienced of Ontario's early aviators and acted as instructor, mechanic, and engineer for the fledgling company. Courtesy, Ontario City Library, Model Colony History Room

in its southern section and beautiful homes north of the downtown area. Ontario had a modern transportation system, modern police and fire departments, and a growing industrial base. And even though it was yet to become apparent, the municipal airport begun by Archie Mitchell was destined to become the nucleus of Ontario's future growth.

The Board of Education maintained a first-rate school district that by the 1930s included elementary schools and the Chaffey Unified High School District, which taught young people from nearly all of the small cities in the area.

The area offered a nearly complete blend of cultural, educational, religious, and social opportunities. In addition, Ontario's first industry, packing and marketing fruit, was thriving. By the 1930s Ontario offered an ideal balance between rural and urban amenities.

In the mid-1880s Abraham Oakley purchased a 10-acre site at the northwest corner of J Street and Euclid Avenue where he planted orange trees and built a handsome home. The family is seen here against the backdrop of Chaffey College and the San Gabriel Mountains. Courtesy, Ontario City Library, Model Colony History Room

The Fruit Industry Matures

Ontario more than fulfilled its destiny to become an agricultural community as George Chaffey had planned it. At the height of its agricultural production, from the late 1920s through the 1940s, the area produced lemons, oranges, limes, guavas, strawberries, blackberries, raspberries, peaches, pears, apricots, cherries, plums, olives, grapes, alfalfa, sugar beets, figs, apples, walnuts, nectarines, and persimmons, as well as numerous varieties of vegetables.

For the most part the climate was ideal. But Southern California's weather vagaries sometimes brought near disaster to the crop growers. Drought, Santa Ana winds, and frost provided the greatest challenges, but pest control also tested the novice fruit growers' mettle.

Two huge storms in December of 1887 nearly brought the colony to its knees. The winds damaged every building in Ontario, totally destroying some homes and most of the young citrus and deciduous orchards. Publicity about the disaster marked the almost instant slow down of the land boom for the colony. Few colonists gave up, however. They learned from the lesson, building better and sturdier structures and planting rows of eucalyptus trees for windbreaks.

It was 1933 before another storm of such proportions hit the area, with winds clocked at between 65 and 75 miles per hour. Five years later a three-week-long cold spell hit in January with temperatures as low as 21 degrees Fahrenheit. On January 21 the daily high temperature was 34 degrees. There were other cold spells,

enough so that methods of warming the orchards were developed. Oil-burning heaters called smudge pots were the primary method, and the oily smoke blackened the sky. In 1937 visibility was so low from the smudge pots that school was cancelled. Two people died and seven were seriously injured because of accidents during the smudging operations. Overall crop loss was estimated to be as high as 40 percent.

In 1938 Ontario experienced massive flooding, and both the San Antonio and Cucamonga washes filled. Boulders the size of houses moved across the landscape and down the alluvial fans. Ontario was completely isolated, and crop loss for the second year in a row was devastating to the economy. Many orchards had to be completely replaced, and whole sections of vineyards were replanted.

The first citrus groves were relatively free of disease. But it was only a matter of time before the scale insects, especially the cottony-cushion scale from Australia, threatened many groves with extinction. Growers tried many remedies for the problem, including the use of all sorts of nasty decoctions containing tobacco, whale oil soap, and coal oil. Fumigation with hydrocyanic acid proved to be the most effective treatment, but was still less than satisfactory. Grove burning, though a drastic measure, was another common solution to scale-infested orchards. Grove owners voluntarily set fire to whole sections of their infested trees to prevent the spread of the insects into healthy trees. But it was a biological solution that eventually saved the groves. The Australian

Vedalia beetle proved to be the scale's natural enemy, and within 18 months of the beetle's introduction in 1888, "California groves were virtually free of the pest," according to Harry W. Lawton and Lewis G. Weathers in "The Origins of Citrus Research in California." Another result of the scale infestation was that California became the first state to pass quarantine laws, in 1888.

Growers in the Southern California citrus belt were aggressive experimenters in irrigating, planting, pruning, harvesting, and managing their crops. They eagerly exchanged information at the numerous fruit and citrus fairs throughout the region and flooded the College of Agriculture at the University of California, Berkeley, with letters requesting information. While citrus historians have called the early pioneers in the citrus belt "abysmally ignorant" when they embarked on their dreams, they did not stay that way.

Citrus

With a strong relationship with Riverside, the first citrus colony in Southern California, Ontario quite willingly experimented in planting slow-growing citrus along with more sensible and more rapidly maturing deciduous fruits. George Chaffey's father had a citrus grove in Riverside, and Chaffey's brother, Dr. Elswood Chaffey, followed suit in Ontario.

Until the completion of the Southern Pacific rail line, fruit grown in Southern California was limited to local use. In the 1870s fruit was transported by wagon to Los Angeles and from there by ship and rail to San Francisco. In 1883, the year of Ontario's founding, the first shipments of citrus from California arrived on the East Coast.

After the Santa Fe line opened in 1885 the industry boomed, with an average profit of between $800 and $1,000 per acre, with some growers realizing up to $3,000 per acre. In 1889 Ontario planted its first navel oranges, and in 1890 the first full season

of citrus was harvested, netting $38,500.

During the planting season in 1890, 630 acres were planted with citrus fruit trees. In 1891 another 658 acres were added, and 21 carloads of oranges and lemons left Ontario packinghouses by rail.

Oranges had to be shipped completely dry, as any moisture on them caused decay. At the same time, the fruit had to be shipped clean. While machines were developed to brush the dust from the oranges once they reached the packinghouse, sometimes the fruit needed a good washing and therefore a good drying. It was a laborious and inefficient process until George Stamm, the son of Godfrey T. Stamm of the Ontario Land and Improvement Company, patented a drying machine in 1915. The device consisted of absorbent material and the means for keeping the fruit rolling over a heating element. Stamm connected an ordinary house furnace with a rotary oil burner so that the heat could be regulated over a distance of 60 feet. To cut down on fire danger, the oil drum was kept buried in the ground far from the packing plant, and no more than a pint of oil was inside the packinghouse at any one time.

Stamm also invented an orange boxing device with a collapsible guard that held the oranges away from the end of the box as the cover was moved down. Over the years he and L.F. Woods, manager of Mountain View Orange and Lemon Growers packinghouse, made many improvements in the citrus packing process.

Deciduous Fruits—
The Dried Fruit Capital

While citrus was the colony's primary crop in its later years, fast-growing deciduous fruits were its mainstay for the first two decades. Ontario Nursery owner D.A. Shaw reported that by August 1884 there were 40,000 peach trees, 29,000 pear trees, 15,000 seedling apple trees, 16,000 grafted

FACING PAGE, TOP: The 1890s saw a number of citrus growers associations formed in the Ontario area. One of these was the Citrus Fruit Association of Ontario, whose packinghouse in west Ontario is shown here. Courtesy, Ontario City Library, Model Colony History Room

FACING PAGE, BOTTOM: A terrible windstorm wreaked havoc in the western portion of San Bernardino County on December 10, 1887. H.J. Rose's drug store was flattened, but the second story, a popular meeting hall, fell to the ground intact. It was later moved to the southeast corner of Euclid Avenue and C Street where it was used as an Episcopal Church for many years. Courtesy, Ontario City Library, Model Colony History Room

apple trees, 1,000 cherry trees, and 16,000 grape cuttings set out in orchards and vineyards.

Though refrigeration cars made rail shipment of fresh fruits possible, drying and canning of the products was by far the most practical way of getting them to market. In 1888 local marketers Rannels and Freeman shipped 100 boxes of apricots to San Diego County. In 1889 C.H. Dyar opened the Ontario Wholesale Fruit Depot in Los Angeles. His outfit handled fresh fruits in season and dried fruits the rest of the year.

On July 16, 1890, the first carload of dried apricots left Ontario for Chicago. Local growers raised funds to form the Ontario Fruit and Produce Company in 1892, which operated an evaporator plant in North Ontario at the Santa Fe line. In August 1893 Sutliff and Groom leased the cannery and evaporator and hired 125 men, women, and children to prepare the fruit for canning and drying. In November of the following year, Sutliff and Groom sent off Ontario's first full trainload of solid fruit. Seventeen carloads containing 408,000 pounds of canned fruits, fresh mixed fruits, raisins, and prunes made their way to Cedar Rapids, Iowa, for distribution in East Coast markets.

The event was cause for a major celebration with a band in full uniform and hundreds of local residents on hand to hear speeches from local and Santa Fe officials. Each car carried a bouquet of chrysanthemums, and on the outside of each was a lithograph of the city of Ontario, decorated with banners bearing shippers' names, palm trees, pampas grass plumes, and other plants and flowers. The last car, decorated by Mrs. M.W. Groom, announced "Sutliff and Groom" in varied colors of mums. Under their brand name, Hawkeye, she created a hawk's head, also in mums. Wreaths of roses flanked the hawk.

Dried fruit stored well and shipped

well and was the most common and logical, if somewhat laborious, preservation method available to the early colonists. It took five pounds of fresh fruit to make one pound of dried. Grapes were cut in bunches and laid out on trays to be turned only once in the process. Prunes were also easy, being allowed to dry on the trees. Apricots required cutting, pitting, fumigating with sulphur to preserve their color, and six days of sun drying. Large camps were established in the open fields, and the pitters often lived with their work until the crop was shipped. Eventually some of the canning and packing houses introduced evaporators, and among the improvements for handling the fruit were inventions coming from agriculture professors at Chaffey College.

The peach pit became an important byproduct of peach processing. It was used as fuel, burned to make charcoal as a purifying agent, and used to make denatured alcohol. In 1907 freestone pits sold for five dollars per ton for fuel. People had been warned to stock up early because a Los Angeles alcohol firm was buying them up fast.

To remove pits, the workers used a fruit-cutting knife to first score the fruit to the pit, then a curved knife was inserted in the stem end of the peach and turned around to remove the pit. It was a time-consuming and thankless task, and one mechanical pitting machine after another was invented. In 1922 Riversider George Wilcox finally came up with a good, practical machine.

In 1925 the California Canning Machinery Company of Ontario took over the manufacture of the Wilcox pitter. According to one board member, W. J. Schaefer, the pitting machine produced 10 to 15 boxes more cut fruit per worker than by the old hand method. The machine still needed perfecting, however, and it wasn't until 1929 that the company came up with a pitter that canners could not fault.

ABOVE: One of San Bernardino County's largest shipments of fruit left Ontario on November 4, 1893. The shipment, put together by the Sutliff and Groom Company, consisted of 408,000 pounds of fruit in 17 railroad cars.

LEFT: Prior to the development of the canning process, the only means of preserving deciduous fruit was through drying. Large wooden trays of fruit were set out in the fields or near the railroad tracks to dry. Many of the growers established camps where the pitters lived until the season was over.

Photos courtesy, Ontario City library, Model Colony History Room

Along with citrus and deciduous trees, settlers planted alfalfa and various grain crops. In this photo the field being harvested is on the future site of Stamm's Bank Block, built in 1887. The Ontario Hotel is visible in the distance. Courtesy, Ontario City Library, Model Colony History Room

Sugar Beets

Chino Rancho owner Richard Gird, who was developing a townsite on his land, signed a contract in December 1891 with Henry and James Oxnard to build a sugar factory. This development meant employment for Ontario residents as well as new farming opportunities. The first sugar beets were planted in February 1891, and the first sugar from that planting of nearly 4,000 acres was manufactured the same year. The factory operated until 1917, when it closed for lack of interest on the part of farmers and ranchers to continue growing sugar beets as other crops and land uses became more lucrative.

Field Labor

Ontario's agricultural labor pool has included numerous ethnic groups, among them Chinese, Japanese, Filipino, Italian,

Dust Bowl migrant workers, and most recently immigrants from Mexico. Then, as now, the citrus, raisin, and deciduous fruit industries are labor intensive only part of the year. Because the growers are hard put in any era to make a profit on their crops, an abundant and inexpensive labor source to harvest and pack the fruit is essential.

Chinese workers were the first major labor force to be employed by Ontario orchard and vineyard owners. Paul Wormser, in an article in *Wong Ho Leun: An American Chinatown*, states that "throughout the 1880s and 1890s, Chinese agriculture labor was a vital element in the success of the interior Southern California Citrus Belt."

Tens of thousands of Chinese had come to America to make their fortunes in "Gold Mountain," as they called California's gold fields, only to be discriminated against and kept, usually by force and threats, from the mines. Their skills ranged from agriculture to stone working, and they provided a ready-made labor force for the railroads and agriculture. They were also highly organized through a Chinese-developed contracting system that has since been used by almost every other ethnic group to perform similar agricultural chores. The vast majority of Chinese laborers worked through a Chinese labor contractor who had up to several hundred workers under his control. During the packing season, growers approached the contractor and made an agreement to have the crop picked and packed. Generally the labor contractor, who was responsible for ensuring that the job was completed, employed a foreman to oversee the job. Workers were usually paid directly by the contractor. "To growers faced with high marketing costs as well as frequently exorbitant shipping rates, having the Chinese in the field often meant the difference between profit and loss," according to Wormser.

By the 1890s there was a large and thriving Chinese settlement in North Ontario (later Upland). The Chinese had practiced citriculture for thousands of years before it was introduced to this country, and it is believed that they introduced many of the practices and techniques still used in the citrus industry. For instance, in the early days of citrus harvesting, the fruit was pulled from the stem, often leaving tears in the skin and making the fruit susceptible to early rot. The use of the citrus clipper to snip the fruit off at the stem and prevent damage made a sudden appearance in the 1880s along with the Chinese laborers. Further evidence that the Chinese may have introduced the citrus clipper comes from a monograph written by Han Yen-chi in A.D. 1178:

Use a small scissors for removing the fruit from the branches, cutting them off even with the surface of the skin and carefully placing them in a basket. To protect them from injury one must be very careful for fear that the skins be cut, causing the volatile oil to escape, when the fruit will easily spoil.

Prior to the advent of packinghouses and the invention of mechanical fruit-sizing methods, packing was done in the field. The Chinese packing method, by far the most efficient of early field packing methods, allowed for sizing the fruit by eye. The skilled packer could fill a crate with odd sizes of fruit and still have the box even at the top.

In spite of Chinese contributions to American labor and culture, by the mid-1870s anti-Chinese feeling abounded. Chinese workers were employed in the inland area of Southern California at odds with statewide bias and even, at times, at great risk of retribution from local residents. In spite of their many contributions, an exclusionary act was passed in 1892. The Geary Act marked the gradual end of Chinese labor in the Citrus Belt, although many Chinese laborers managed to hang on to jobs in the area. By the mid-1920s most Ontario and inland area Chinese settlements were ghost towns and memories.

The exclusion of the Chinese created hardship for growers throughout the state, and as early as 1880 Japanese labor was being brought in to work in the fields. By 1910 there were more than 72,000 Japanese workers in California. As a labor force, they soon monopolized sugar beet production and the berry cultivation industry. Ontario growers welcomed them as they had the Chinese before. Unlike the Chinese, however, the Japanese began to acquire land. Even though it was poor land for agriculture, they managed to reclaim it and produce crops. Unfortunately, as landowners the Japanese were perceived as a threat because they were no longer inexpensive day laborers.

Another cheap labor force came from a seemingly unlikely source, and from 1907 until 1910 Hindustani workers

ABOVE: The Mitchell and Butterfield packing company operated out of an old livery stable. The building was built in the Victorian Gothic style and later became the home of the Hotpoint factory. Courtesy, Ontario City Library, Model Colony History Room

RIGHT: A co-op cannery organization was established in the fall of 1915 under the name of the San Antonio Growers Association. The Ontario plant, shown here, was built on the east side of Campus Avenue near the Union Pacific tracks. The cannery was in operation by July 1916 and was a great success. Courtesy, Ontario City Library, Model Colony History Room

clad in turbans appeared on the migrant worker scene. The Hindus, like the Japanese, soon drifted into the category of land owners and farmers.

Many of the area's Armenian families also came to Ontario as migrant farm workers. Among the other ethnic groups that came to California and put down roots, first as field workers and then landowners, were the Portuguese, Italians, and Swiss. These immigrants added great land holdings and knowledge to the local viticulture.

The first wave of Mexican migrant workers lasted from 1914 through 1934. Early in the development of the colony, Ontarians employed Mexican labor along with the Chinese to clear the land and prepare it for building or planting. The Ontario growers made great use of Mexican workers in all phases of growing, harvesting, and processing their fruit. Entire families worked together, camping near the fields at night.

The last major immigrant labor force used in Ontario were the Filipinos. Unlike other groups of laborers, however, the Filipinos wasted no time in organizing, and by 1934 they had formed the Filipino Labor Union. Unfortunately, the result of unionizing was that growers found them too costly and too willing to go on strike, preferring laborers from Mexico who could more easily be controlled by the threat of deportation.

Cooperatives and Exchanges

As the fruit industry matured, an adjunct marketing industry sprang up. At first, according to Rahno Mabel MacCurdy in *The History of the California Fruit Growers Exchange,*

. . . the system of dealer purchase, as imperfect as it was, returned profits both to the grower and dealer, but as the supply increased, business proved more remunerative and more uncertain. Also there was no understanding between the buyers as to distribution among the eastern markets, and glutting and undersupply followed.

Initially, crops were purchased based on estimates of the value of fruit still on the trees. Later, buyers bargained for the crop, paying "a stated price per packed box and doing the packing and shipping, and generally the picking," according to MacCurdy. Orchard owners soon tired of this method of getting their crops to market. They increasingly netted less than the cost of packing and shipping. According to Lawton and Weathers in "The Origins of Citrus Research in California," "Fruit often 'bunched up' in warehouses or during shipment and rotted. Crooked commission agents and auction dealers found numerous ways to fleece the owners of profits . . . the railroad established ruthlessly exorbitant shipping rates."

Both the citrus and deciduous fruit growers found that unfair marketing practices on the part of commissioners were cheating them out of most of their profits. As a result the growers began to form cooperative ventures for their own protection.

MacCurdy cites a letter (carefully leaving out the buyer's name) from a Southern California grower, James Barnhill, concerning the buyers' methods

. . . that would enable them to reject any amount they wished as they were the judges as to what was merchantable. I remember one year in the late eighties I sold my crop to [name deleted]. He was to pay me one-and-three-fourths cents per pound, delivered to his packing house. After delivering three or four loads I asked to be shown how they had graded out and found they had thrown out fifty percent as unmerchantable . . . I insisted that I be allowed to take my discarded oranges home—hired a small grader, engaged a good packer. I graded the fruit and nailed the boxes myself and shipped them local freight . . . to San Francisco and got a better net price for the discarded oranges than paid me.

"Growers realized that the job of creating better distribution methods was theirs, and they organized to bring about the

ABOVE: Clifford C. Graber, founder of Graber Olive House, arrived in Ontario with his brother Charles in 1892. Clifford began curing olives as a hobby. Today, Graber's is the oldest business still in existence in Ontario. Courtesy, Ontario City Library, Model Colony History Room

RIGHT: Citrus packers were able to wrap and pack about 70 boxes of oranges per day. Workers wore gloves while packing to protect the fruit from scratches and bruises. Courtesy, Ontario City Library, Model Colony History Room

necessary marketing improvements," according to the U.S. Department of Agriculture Farmers Cooperative Service bulletin "The Sunkist Adventure." The growers found relief through grower-owned cooperatives. Several emerged in the late 1880s that will serve as examples.

The first united action taken by the growers to combat the agency and commissioner gouging took place at a meeting on October 24, 1885, in Los Angeles, and the Orange Growers Protective Union of Southern California was formed. The purpose of the union was to regulate shipments to keep markets from being overstocked. The union lasted until 1893, but because it had tried to represent the interests of both packers and growers, internal friction coupled with the opposition of buyers and commissioners led to its demise.

Ontario growers were among the first to organize, although the first truly cooperative association was organized in 1888 in Riverside. Known as the Pachappa Orange Growers Association, it initially operated through the F.B. Devine Packinghouse. By 1893 it had its own packinghouse and had developed its grower contracts to where they requested that all fruit grown by members be graded, packed, and sold under association management on a variety pool basis.

Just as Ontario orchards were beginning to produce in the 1890s, the marketing crisis for growers reached its peak.

Following the Pachappa pattern, a group of Ontario deciduous and citrus growers formed the Ontario Fruit Exchange on June 3, 1893, and in September the group associated with the San Antonio Fruit Exchange in Pomona. Two years later Ontario withdrew from San Antonio to become part of the Southern California Fruit Exchange, thus becoming an association of the Ontario-Cucamonga district of the Southern California Fruit Exchange.

In addition to the Ontario Fruit Exchange, which initially included both deciduous and citrus growers, several other groups of exclusively citrus growers organized. One such was the Citrus Fruit Association of Ontario, formed in 1893.

Over the years many of these early exchanges fell by the wayside or merged to form larger groups. Two of the most powerful of the larger groups were the California Citrus Union and the previously mentioned Southern California Fruit Exchange.

Numerous transitions and internecine haggling led to the formation of the California Fruit Agency, a merger of the Southern California Fruit Exchange and California Citrus Union, a short-lived organization of shippers. A basic tenet of the exchange philosophy was for local control, and members believed the directors did not consult with them properly.

Under duress, the agency was dissolved in September 1904 in favor of exchange operations. By the next year incorporation as the California Fruit Growers Exchange was complete. In 1908 the California Fruit Growers adopted the Sunkist trademark as part of its marketing campaign. In 1952, to better match its internationally recognized trademark, the exchange changed its corporate name to Sunkist Growers, Inc. The basic cooperative principles adopted in 1905 have had a lasting effect on the cooperative now known as Sunkist Growers, Inc., since its formation.

Ontario has played a significant role in the development and growth of the citrus growers' clout in the marketplace, particularly in the manufacturing and producing of citrus by-products, and became the location for the Sunkist by-products plant.

Other Agricultural Industries
By the end of the 1890s it had become evident that the marketing of all the fresh fruit grown was economically impossible. By 1914 several attempts had been made to make use of the citrus culls, fruit which failed to meet aesthetic and size standards, but was otherwise healthy. Thomas

One of Euclid Avenue's early business establishments was Armstrong Nurseries, founded by John S. Armstrong in the early 1890s. In 1904 he moved his business to the east side of Euclid Avenue between C and D streets. The nurseries remained at that location until December 1956 when a new facility was opened. Courtesy, Ontario City Library, Model Colony History Room

Crawford, Inc., started manufacturing marmalade, and later operated as Exchange Orange Products Company in Ontario until 1920, when the high cost of producing its single product forced the company out of business. That same year a new company, also called Exchange Orange Products, was incorporated as a cooperative by former stockholders in the original Exchange Orange Products Company, who were also members of the Sunkist group. In 1931 Sunkist purchased all outstanding stock, and Exchange Orange Products Company became a wholly owned subsidiary of Sunkist.

In 1958 the Exchange Orange Products Company merged with Sunkist Growers, Inc., and Exchange Lemon Products Company. In 1983 both the lemon processing plant, which was located in Corona, and the Ontario orange processing plant were combined. The main Sunkist plant for processing lemon and orange by-products is still in Ontario.

Besides citrus and deciduous fruit, Ontario has also been home to other agricultural products. Two of the best known companies in this field are Graber Olive and Armstrong Nurseries.

The Mediterranean climate is ideal for olives, one of the world's oldest cultivated crops. When Clifford and Charles Graber arrived in Ontario in 1892, the Pomona Valley was already the leading olive producing area in North America. The brothers bought a 10-acre lot, put in a grove of oranges, and planted the rows in between with berries and row crops.

Though they didn't grow olives, Clifford did pick some from neighboring trees and pickled them according to a recipe he had. He included the cured olives with the produce he and his brother grew and made a hobby of finding the definitive olive recipe. He eventually acquired one he liked from the University of California, Davis, and tinkered with it until he was satisfied.

The brothers dissolved their partnership. Clifford maintained his orange grove as his primary income and grew olives as a hobby. Finding the perfect olive for his perfect recipe led him to develop a number of firsts for the industry. Until Graber became concerned about size, there were no standards. He invented a grader that worked so well that he built seven more. In 1929, after a busy life in the community, serving on the Chaffey Union High School Board of Trustees and as a city councilman from 1918 to 1925, he decided to go into olive production full time. The Graber mail-order business he founded has become world famous. It is Ontario's oldest business and is still operated by the Graber family. While the Graber olive ranch is in Lindsay, California, the olives are still cured, canned, and sold out of the original Fourth Street site.

Armstrong Nurseries, founded in the early 1890s by John S. Armstrong, was one of Ontario's first landmarks. Armstrong began by providing local farmers with eucalyptus trees used for wind breaks. He later added deciduous and eventually citrus stock. The nursery developed an international reputation, shipping plants to such places as Russia, Palestine, Spain, and Morocco. The Ontario City Library now occupies the site of Armstrong's first location.

In 1904 the nursery was moved to the southeast corner of D Street and Euclid, and it was from there that Armstrong gained international recognition for his plant breeding program. He developed the Robertson navel orange and a seedless Valencia orange. His first wife's name graces one of the most famous roses of all time—the Charlotte Armstrong—which won All American Rose Honors in 1941. The Charlotte Armstrong rose is also Ontario's official city flower. In 1943 Armstrong's Mirandy rose also earned All American Rose Honors.

The nursery moved from its historic location on Euclid in 1956 to Mountain Avenue and Fourth Street. By 1964 the nursery boasted 700 acres at various locations and had sales yards at North Hollywood, Culver City, and Long Beach. There is still an Armstrong Garden Center at Mountain and Fourth.

The Wine Tradition

Ontario's grape and wine industry very nearly equalled the citrus industry in size, success, and international recognition. The threads of this continent's two winemaking traditions came together in Ontario's vineyards.

Ranchero Tiburcio Tapia is believed to have planted the first vineyard in the Ontario-Cucamonga area. Tapia's majordomo, Jose Valdez, ran the winery. The buildings, located at Foothill and Vineyard, are still in use today. In Tapia's day, Vineyard was the site of a rushing stream, and the ranchero used a water wheel to turn the grape crusher. John Rains, who later owned the rancho, furthered the winemaking tradition and planted more acres of grapes.

Through land purchases from Captain Joseph Garcia, George Chaffey acquired much of that ancient vineyard and continued the legacy. Chaffey hired German-born John Klusman to work in the vineyards, and by 1896 Klusman had his own vineyards and sold his first harvest to Chaffey for six dollars per ton. In 1900 Klusman teamed up with land speculator Colonel Morton E. Post to invest in more vineyards and to build a winery.

Every Sunday during the 1880s and 1890s Italian immigrant Secondo Guasti drove from Los Angeles to look at the land near Ontario and dream of planting a vineyard. He worked and saved his money, and in 1900 he purchased 4,000 acres and began the planting that would be the foundation of his Italian Vineyard Company. Ultimately Guasti built a Roman-style villa that became the center of a patriarchal colony complete with a church, a school, and a farm operation large enough

to support his family and his workers. His holding tanks contained five million gallons of wine at the height of the operation. The Italian Vineyard Company buildings are located at the edge of Ontario International Airport along the Southern Pacific tracks.

On the East Coast, Dr. Frank Garrett formed Garrett and Company Winery in Medoc, North Carolina, in 1835. A nephew, Paul Garrett (nicknamed Cap'n Garrett), built the business into an international success. Seeking a site from which to develop a white wine, Paul Garrett sent his nephew to California, where he purchased vineyards on Haven Avenue, north of the Santa Fe tracks and south of the spectacular Mission Winery at Haven and Foothill that had been created by Post and Klusman. In 1912 Paul Garrett came to California, fell in love with the buildings and the land, and leased them for Garrett and Company.

In 1916 San Bernardino County voted to outlaw the sale of alcohol. And in 1918, two years before the Eighteenth Amendment was approved, Klusman and Post happily sold out to Garrett. Garrett had already begun making his white wine and, in search of a name for it and his new operation, he decided to name both for the first white child born in America—Virginia Dare.

After repeal of the Eighteenth Amendment in 1933, Garrett and Company expanded rapidly. Guasti's empire, however, failed to survive the death of its founder in 1927 and the death of his son in 1933, and it was bought out by Horace Lanza, a former member of the grape growers cooperative Fruit Industries. He was unable to get the Italian Vineyard Company back on its feet, and in 1943 Garrett bought the former Guasti lands and buildings. Garrett put up billboards proclaiming Virginia Dare winery to be the world's most beautiful winery and the vineyard to be the world's largest. No one disputed the claim.

ABOVE: The Italian Vineyard Company, founded by Secondo Guasti in 1900, remained in the Guasti family until the death of Secondo, Jr., in 1933. Grapes harvested from Guasti's nearby vineyards were brought to the IVC winery where they were made into wine by workers who lived in the company town of Guasti. Courtesy, Ontario City Library, Model Colony History Room

LEFT: At the State Citrus Fair, held in Los Angeles in 1891, Ontario's exhibit featured the famous gravity mule car. A full-size streetcar was adorned with fruit and incorporated life-size model horses standing on the rear platform. The exhibit attracted much attention for Ontario and received "honorable mention" in the "most artistic display of citrus fruits" class. Courtesy, Ontario City Library, Model Colony History Room

*By 1940 the Ontario General Electric plant was pro-
ducing more than one million irons per year. Beginning with the 20-millionth, produced in June 1941,
the plant started the tradition of presenting a gold-
plated commemorative iron to a prominent individual. On November 14, 1956, Ronald Reagan, host
of the "General Electric Theater" television program,
received the 50-millionth flatiron. Courtesy, Ontario
City Library, Model Colony History Room*

New Directions

Perhaps the most symbolic indication of the colony's maturity was the fading away of the Ontario Land and Improvement Company. After 1890 the only apparent activity the company engaged in was a few farming projects and the sale of unimproved lands. Colonel Oliver S. Picher, one of the original board members, died in 1895. The remaining active board members were Charles Frankish and Godfrey T. Stamm. That year an outside real estate firm was hired to dispose of the remaining land. In 1906 an ammendment was filed to the articles of incorporation, reducing the number of directors to three. In 1912 the corporation was suspended and reorganized as the Frankish Company. Charles Frankish retired in 1927, after 41 years of dedication to developing Ontario and Upland.

The passing of the Land and Improvement Company marked the end of the colony days. In 1910 the town of Ontario opted to call itself the City of Ontario, when it became a fifth-class city eligible to develop wards and elect a city council.

In 1898 George Chaffey returned to Ontario in time to help solve a water crisis brought on by the area's rapid growth and a period of drought. In 1901 USC trustees, in an effort to gain control of the Chaffey Trust, tried to merge Chaffey College with the university. Chaffey filed suit to account for the funds he had provided, forcing the formation of a new board of trustees and the university's relinquishing all claims to the property.

The Chaffey family continued to have a significant impact on developments in Southern California.

As soon as George Chaffey was through helping with the water problems in Ontario, he reconsidered the possibility of irrigating the Imperial Valley. Within four years of his return from Australia, he had made a fortune by irrigating more than a million acres of desert. He is considered the father of El Centro, California, and Calexico, Mexico, just across the border.

Financially secure, Chaffey returned to Ontario and bought the *Ontario Record-Observer* in 1902, and changed the paper's name to the *Record*. With his son Andrew he purchased the Ontario State Bank and renamed it the First National Bank of Ontario.

Andrew Chaffey was a brilliant pioneer in the banking industry. With his father's financing, he eventually opened the First National Bank of Upland and became president of the Hibernian Bank of Los Angeles, which was eventually renamed the California Bank, another of his father's investments. One of Andrew Chaffey's most notable accomplishments was introducing the branch banking system to California.

Among George Chaffey's other accomplishments is building the irrigation system for East Whittier and La Habra near Los Angeles. In 1905 George and his brother Charles ventured into the Owens Valley in an attempt to gain the water rights there to turn the valley into an agricultural empire. The City of Los Angeles had also sent representatives to the valley for water rights.

A long and drawn out court battle decided that the Chaffeys and the City of Los Angeles would each get half of the Owens Valley water rights. The Chaffeys ultimately sold their interests in the valley to Los Angeles.

In many ways, Ontario and its founder prospered together in the beginning

ABOVE: North Ontario, originally part of the Ontario Colony lands, changed its name to Upland in 1902 and incorporated as a city in 1906. Second Avenue is the commercial center of the original town and still houses many businesses. Although some of the facades and store fronts have changed, many of the buildings seen in this 1918 photo are still standing. Courtesy, Ontario City Library, Model Colony History Room

RIGHT: Charles Frankish began to develop the South Side Tract in early 1887. Main Street, shown here around 1890, ran parallel to the Southern Pacific tracks, thus drawing commercial interests away from Euclid Avenue. Located on this street were Stamm's Bank Block, with the AOUW "Opera House" and a stables and carriage barn to the east. Courtesy, Ontario City Library, Model Colony History Room

years of the twentieth century. Both experienced growth and change, and by 1906 Ontario, already psychologically divided into North and South Ontario, was split into two different cities.

North Ontario Becomes Upland

As early as 1888 the settlement of North Ontario—later to become Upland—wanted a separate identity, but when the matter of incorporation came to a vote it was defeated. North Ontario developed its own townsite and its own identity, and when Ontario annexed more land to its city limits in 1901, the boundaries went just to the edge of the townsite. As a result North Ontario had to move its post office to the north side of G Street to keep it inside the townsite.

Over the next few years interests in North Ontario carried on heated debate concerning the boundaries. In 1902 North Ontario successfully petitioned the supervisors for a name change from North Ontario to Upland. Finally, on May 5, 1906, an incorporation election for Upland was held with 183 voting for incorporation and 19 against.

Boundary disputes continued into 1935, when on March 21 an annexation election was held that essentially restored Upland boundaries to the original tracts laid out in the previous century. Technically, this made Upland larger than Ontario, though Ontario's population was two-thirds greater.

Business and Industrial Accomplishments

Although overshadowed by the fast and well-publicized development of the agricultural industries, Ontario's business and industrial developments from the beginning of the colony were considerable. In fact, this early business and industrial precedent allowed Ontario to maintain a substantial economic base during two economic disasters, the Great Depression nationally and the loss of the fruit industry locally.

Within four years of its founding, On-

Andrew McCord Chaffey, George's son, is possibly the best known of the Chaffey descendants. In 1902 George and Andrew took over the Ontario State Bank and reorganized it as the First National Bank of Ontario. Andrew went on to become president of the California Bank and introduced the concept of branch banking to the state. Courtesy, Ontario City Library, Model Colony History Room

tario had a sizable business district. A few of the businesses established in the first 10 years continued into the 1980s. By 1885 the colony boasted a burgeoning population along with a hotel, two grocery stores, a dry goods store, a furniture store, a confectionary, a book and notions store, a restaurant, a general hardware store, a paint shop, a butcher shop, a boarding house, a barber shop, a harness shop, a blacksmith, a carpenter, a livery stable, a bakery, and a drugstore.

By the end of the year, William J. Waddington, Ontario's architect and builder, had set up a planing mill to make such housebuilding necessities as doors, blinds, sashes, and cabinets. Waddington's father, Joseph, built a grain warehouse. Other new businesses got a start, including a millinery and a second drugstore.

In 1887 the two-story bank block was completed at the southwest corner of Main and Euclid. It housed a bank, stores, and the new post office site.

Businesses that had signs up on Godfrey Stamm's business building included the Ontario State Bank, "S.P. Hildreth, President. Capital $50,000," as well as a billiards parlor that billed itself as a "a temperate,

orderly place of amusement"; P.D. Gazzola, barber, "Hot and Cold Water always on hand. Ladies! Bring your scissors to be sharpened"; Miller's Dry Goods; Robert Smart, Ontario Boot and Shoe Store, "Shoes that Wear"; and R. Hickman, Grocer, "The leading house in Ontario."

In the next few years, several business blocks were built, including the Freeman, Friend, and Brooks blocks. And in 1891 William B. Collins, C.R. Sykes, C.E. Harwood, William Friend, L.S. Dyar, J.C. Lynch, and James Young formed a board of trade to promote Ontario products and businesses.

Draper's mortuary, still in business in 1989, started in 1900 when the colony's tailor, L.B. Draper, bought out undertaker Fred Clarke. And in 1900 Draper bought out S.R. Lippincott, of Lippincott and Garbutt, undertakers and embalmers. In addition to the undertaking business, Lippincott also sold artists' supplies and pictures. Draper expanded the undertaking business as the town expanded, and his fancy white hearse was the first in the region.

But business and industry were not the only areas of growth in Ontario in the early part of the century. From 1900 until the market crash in 1929, social services such as law enforcement and medicine grew at a rapid pace.

The Medical Community

From the beginning Ontario and Upland attracted first-rate medical doctors. The first was George Chaffey's brother, Doctor Elswood Chaffey. In 1885 Ontario's first woman doctor, Idris Gregory, set up practice. And in 1896 the Craig family moved into North Ontario. This family of physicians, headed by Doctor William H. Craig, left a lasting impact on the quality of medical care Ontario and Upland residents receive to this day. The older Craigs had eight children, four of whom became doctors. All stayed on to practice medicine, and in one case dentistry, in Ontario and Upland. To distinguish the young Craigs one from the other and from their father "Old Doctor Craig," they all became known by their first names: Doctor John, Doctor Mary, Doctor Step, and Doctor Bun, the dentist.

Legends and stories abound about Dr. Mary, who would haul her son, later dermatologist Doctor Craig Williamson of Pasadena, on her hip as she made house calls. One tale has it that when she was stopped for speeding by a traffic officer she looked him up and down and said "Young man, I delivered you, and I'm on my way to deliver another baby," as she stepped on the accelerator and sped off.

In 1907 "Old Dr. Craig" led the movement to build the Ontario-Upland area's first hospital at San Antonio and Arrow. Prior to that he performed surgery in people's homes on their kitchen tables. Stockholders in the first hospital, beside Doctor Craig, were Doctor C. Sheppard, J.B. Draper, Judge J.R. Pollock, Doctor E.W. Reid, P.E. Walline, J.J. Atwood, G.A. Hanson, Harold Moore, and Charles Ruedy.

A second, expanded hospital, San Antonio Community Hospital, was built on the same site in 1924 with $75,000 in seed money donated by Mary Fancis Paul, widow of Colonel James L. Paul. Mrs. Paul died the year before the hospital was completed. Dr. A.A. Aita, the hospital's superintendant for 32 years, created many innovative programs to provide medical care to the entire community regardless of an individual's social or economic status. San Antonio Community Hospital remained the primary medical center for Ontario and Upland until 1951, when Ontario Community Hospital was founded.

The Post Office

Ontario's postal service was established on February 19, 1883, under the guidance of Leopold Alexander. Ontario legend has it that the first post office was set up in a railroad boxcar. Ontario's second postmaster, A.E. Payne, operated the post office out of his grocery store on the corner of I and Euclid. The post office's third site was the Southern Pacific Hotel building, where it remained until December 3, 1895, when the hotel was destroyed by fire. A bookstore in the Ohio block at A Street (now Holt) and Euclid was its next home, and then the Frankish building at Transit and Euclid.

The facility became a third-class post office in 1888 and a second-class post office in 1907. That year (1907) the service began renting its first cancelling machine from the United States government, and in 1909 the post office was raised to a first-class ranking.

The first air mail service was inaugurated in the 1930s. In 1940, using WPA funds, the government erected a handsome Spanish-style structure that was touted as the most modern post office on the Pacific Coast. The postmaster was Carl J. Hase, who served until 1954. Bernhardt Ollila became acting postmaster after Hase, until the appointment in 1956 of Charles F. Linck. Linck's career with the post office lasted until December 31, 1979. He was the last Ontario postmaster to be presidentially appointed.

Law Enforcement

When Ontario was founded in 1882, law enforcement in San Bernardino County was provided by the sheriff's department. The department was headed by John C. King, who eventually became more interested in silver mining (the Bonanza King mine) than in enforcing the law. He was succeeded by Sheriff Francis Holcomb, who had his hands full dealing with train robbers. When Ontario incorporated in 1891, L.J.E. Tyler was elected marshall, thus becoming Ontario's first police officer. He was succeeded the following year by J.B. Southard, who was succeeded by Ed McManus.

Under the leadership of Walter O. Hardy, elected in November 1907, the department expanded. During Hardy's tenure the

Walter O. Hardy, left, was elected Township Constable in November 1907 and remained at that post until 1927 when he was replaced by Arthur Axley, right, who served until 1934. They are seen here in the mid-1920s with a hobo who was "passing through" the town. Courtesy, Ontario City Library, Model Colony History Room

city changed the title from marshall to chief of police. Hardy held the position until 1927, and during his tenure Ontario's first motorcycle officer, Wiley Poindexter, was hired on June 28, 1915. The next police chiefs were forced to resign for mismanagement of the department. On October 7, 1936, J.C. Smith was ousted for allegedly turning the other way while gambling operations continued in the city. Smith had succeeded Arthur Axley in 1934, who was forced to resign after eight years for failing to deal effectively with poultry thefts.

Until radios became common police communications tools, the station kept in contact with officers on patrol by means of red lights mounted on the city's light standards. If the patrol officer saw one light up, he knew to phone in to find out where he was needed. In 1935 one-way radios—from station to car—were installed in police units. Two-way radios were introduced in 1940, and in 1951 three-way radios—station to car to car to station—were implemented.

Unfortunately, Ontario's history also includes episodes of organized racism, which culminated on September 8, 1924, with a huge march of Ku Klux Klan members from downtown Ontario to Chaffey High School. Flames from the burning cross at the school were visible in Upland and downtown Ontario. The event included the swearing in of 150 new Klansmen. School board members came in for some heated criticism for permitting such a gathering on school grounds.

One Ontario resident maintained, "Chaffey High School is maintained by taxes paid by Jews and Catholics. (It does) not seem fair (for) an organization opposed to those people to assemble there."

Board member Thomas Nisbet replied with the same argument that Klan members were also taxpayers and that they expected criticism when they agreed. He said that the board permitted the demonstra-

tion on the grounds that the Klan agreed not to appear in masks. There was only one vigilante action in Ontario that appeared to be Klan related. A group of men took custody of a Los Angeles man who was acting overly friendly toward children in the streets. He was turned over to the police for questioning.

The Great Depression

The stock market crash on October 29, 1929, "Black Tuesday," marked the beginning of America's Great Depression. Economically, Ontario fared somewhat better than other areas; even so, the first two years were rough on the small community. The city did what it could and hired temporary employees for street clean-up and a new free trash pick-up program.

As for agriculture, the Depression served to exacerbate some already existing problems. Prohibition, in effect for more than 10 years, had caused a severe crisis for the area's grape industry, which was just barely keeping its head above water at the time of the crash. With the onset of the Depression, grape growers were even harder pressed to market their products. To meet the challenge of selling tons of grapes formerly destined for the wine industry, the grape industry, with the help of the federal government, came up with numerous new products. With the repeal of the Eighteenth Amendment in 1933, however, local wineries were once again allowed to produce.

Marketing difficulties and a slump in prices already extant in the citrus and deciduous fruit industries only worsened after the economy collapsed. By 1930 growers were disposing of surplus citrus crops in any way they could. But thanks to the existence of the Orange Products Exchange and the rapid development of new orange product lines, the market crash crisis for local growers was much allayed. During the 1930s the Exchange proved to be one of the largest local employers.

The Cal-Aero Flight Academy operated from September 14, 1940, to October 16, 1944. During those years more than 10,000 pilots graduated from the Chino facility, with graduation ceremonies occurring every six weeks. Courtesy, Ontario City Library, Model Colony History Room

By 1932 more than 16 million Americans were out of work. Consequently, there was great antipathy toward cheap foreign labor, especially the Mexican farm workers. At the same time, a flood of out-of-work men and women headed west to California. The situation was made worse in the mid-1930s by the influx of displaced Dust Bowl farmers.

Hundreds of men seeking work lined up and camped on Ontario's Euclid Avenue parkway. Locals needing a hired hand or so for the day would drive up and down the street, honk or holler, and be swamped by eager workers. Some worked for far less than even the meager wages formerly paid to the Mexican workers.

Nature also gave Ontario several poundings during the 1930s. In January 1933 Santa Ana winds clocked at between 65 and 75 miles per hour destroyed as much as one-third of the navel orange crop.

Southern California, whose facilities were already stretched to the breaking point by the masses of transients created by the Depression, was further shaken on March 10, 1933, by the Long Beach earthquake. Thousands of families and businesses were displaced. Ontario and Upland became a major relocation point for an additional homeless population as people fled the earthquake area.

The effects of the 1933 earthquake were felt by the school system for years afterward. The quake was severe enough to cause considerable damage to a number of Ontario structures, not the least of which were those on the Chaffey High School and College campus. All of the high school buildings were condemned. The school district was in terrible financial straits, due in part to the fact that 26 percent of the district's taxes were unpaid. Thanks to an extreme cost- and salary-cutting program, there was just enough money for salaries, and none for building.

In 1937 a severe freeze damaged crops and resulted in as much as a 40 percent loss. The following year, 1938, saw floods almost equal to the great floods in the previous century. Sheets of water flowed off the mountains, tumbling boulders the size of houses through orchards, vineyards, and structures. Four people died in the Canyon and Cucamonga area.

Nevertheless, thanks to hard campaigning on the part of the Ontario Chamber of Commerce and civic leaders, industry continued to develop, housing increased, and many businessmen fleeing other areas moved in and started anew here. By 1935 the estimated municipal population was 15,000, up from the 1910 census of 4,274—a growth of 491 percent. The *Daily Report* also noted that business conditions had improved locally. In fact, nationally business was up by 57 percent of what it had been during the Depression's lowest ebb. Ontario was also on the road to recovery. A *Daily Report* news item stated:

Part of this increase may be attributed by merchants to SERA and WPA payrolls in this community, but in addition a considerable proportion of it has resulted directly from improved agricultural conditions in some lines, and in the maintenance of larger payrolls in local industrial establishments.

The Alphabet Projects

Ontario was quick to take advantage of the various recovery act funding sources made available for improving municipal buildings. Such projects would continue through 1941 with the completion of the Municipal Airport's concrete runway system. Many of the landmark Mission Revival style buildings dotting the landscape today were built during the Depression using SERA (State Emergency Relief Act), PWA (Public Works Administration), and WPA (Work Projects Administration) funds.

School superintendent Gardiner W. Spring was particularly adept at manipulating the federal funding sources. During this period all the high school buildings were replaced and the junior college buildings were put up, including the aeronautics building in 1934, the Chaffey Memorial Library in 1935, the gymnasiums, music building, plunge, and bleachers in 1937, the civic auditorium, which carries Spring's name, in 1939, and the second unit of the aeronautics building in 1941. Most of the facilities, though owned by the junior college, were shared with the high school.

Since 1910 Ontario's first city hall had been housed in the old bankrupt Ontario Country Club, built in 1903 on the site of the former Southern Pacific Hotel, which had burned in 1897. Ontario's second city hall was built with WPA funds in 1936. The Mission Revival style building now houses the city's municipal museum.

John Galvin Park, named for the assistant City Services Manager who had served the city for more than 20 years, also benefitted from WPA funds. When the Wells Fargo-American Express building was razed in 1936, WPA funds paid for moving the used bricks to the park site. There the bricks were used in constructing the new and modern sports amphitheater, which was funded by SERA. A local news article noted that "few of the young generation who use the new amphitheater will realize that the bricks upon which they sit, housed the bags and baggage of their ancestors when they came to Ontario." At one time, the Los Angeles Angels baseball team trained at the park, which featured what was considered to be one of the best municipal baseball diamonds in the country.

Industrial Development
It was during the 1930s that the first signs appeared that Ontario's agriculture industry might be on the way out as a major economic force. Seeing the handwriting on the wall, school curriculum planners began to place more of an emphasis on voca-

tional and business training. Community leaders worked at attracting more industry, a relatively easy job because Ontario was already exporting an impressive number of goods throughout the world. Exports besides agricultural products included concrete pipes, electric power, lineal lumber, electric flatirons, curling irons, heating pads, table stoves, sandwich grills, air heaters, tools, clay pigeons, machinery, and castings and other forge products. Other exports were wine, soybean products, nursery stock, carbonated beverages, canned goods, chemical products, cosmetics, dairy products, feed and grain products, fertilizer, and orchard heaters.

By 1935 local businesses were providing a $2 million annual payroll. Manufacturing plants' physical facilities were valued at $43 million. Community leaders boasted that the West End had a tremendous industrial future.

Another War on the Horizon
Even as the area was making inroads toward economic stability, rumors of pending war in Europe and of Japanese aggression in Asia were causing ripples of uneasiness in America. But isolationist sentiments and the distance of two oceans insulated most from emotional involvement in faraway events. On September 1, 1939, Germany invaded Poland, and on September 3 Britain and France declared war on Germany. President Roosevelt declared a state of limited emergency. The country started gearing up for a war no one believed the United States would have to fight.

During this time Ontario residents carried on with their normal community events. In 1940 the city was excitedly preparing its float entry for the 52nd Annual Pasadena Tournament of Roses Parade, and the college and high school band members were busy practicing for their own Parade participation.

Company G of the West End Unit of the California National Guard was

All States Picnic:
The Longest Picnic Table in the World

The notion of grouping people around tables by state of origin started in 1916 at Ontario Chamber of Commerce annual dinners. For the first 20 years of Ontario's existence, there were no adult residents who were native to the area, and the idea of celebrating one's roots with others from the same state or country was well received. It was a sort of regional reunion, a get together for people from the same part of the country, and an opportunity for strangers and new neighbors to swap stories and reminisce about their common roots.

In 1932, on the 50th anniversary of the Colony's founding, the city threw a big All

States Picnic at the Fourth Street park. City manager Carl Holmer took things a step further and set plans in motion to have an annual All States Picnic under the pepper trees on Euclid Avenue's grassy center.

The first picnic committee chairman was R. Fred Price, and the first annual All States picnic was held on May 20, 1939, the same weekend as the 18th Annual Chaffey Junior Fair. Tables extended more than a mile from E Street to Hawthorne Drive. An estimated 30,000 people attended, and every state in the union was represented, plus Alaska, Hawaii, and Canada.

The tradition was off and running. The second annual

picnic was held in 1940, and the third annual picnic was held in 1941. The picnic was cancelled for the duration of World War II, but resumed in 1948. That year an estimated 120,000 people attended.

Ontario continued the tradition up through the 1960s when interest began to flag, and the 1970s saw the world's longest picnic table fade away.

The All States Picnic attracted thousands of visitors to the Euclid Avenue parkway annually. The event gained notoriety when its "mile long picnic table" was featured in Ripley's Believe It or Not *cartoons. The picnic tradition continued into the 1970s. Courtesy, Ontario City Library, Model Colony History Room*

ABOVE: In the USO's recreational facilities housed in the Frankish building, enlisted men from the Ontario Army Air Field staged an evening's entertainment on March 9, 1945. Soldiers served refreshments while guests danced to the music of an all-soldier orchestra. Courtesy, Ontario City Library, Model Colony History Room

RIGHT: Many Ontario women entered the armed services during World War II. Genevera Faye McQuatters, right, was a graduate of Chaffey High School and a businesswoman in Ontario who enlisted in the WAAC in July 1942. At the end of the war Major McQuatters was the assistant director of the WAAC Service Command at Governor's Island, New York. McQuatters is seen here with Children's Librarian Margaret Hamilton, left, and an unidentified child. Courtesy, Ontario City Library, Model Colony History Room

inducted in January, followed later in the year by the Ontario Unit, Company I, Third Battalion. Ontario also started a Home Guard Unit and passed a city defense ordinance. A group of Ontario women flyers organized themselves into a national defense corps. Numerous young men enlisted, among them Ontario residents Joe and Don Lakin, who were assigned to duty aboard the USS *Arizona* in the Pacific.

All of the features that made Ontario ideal for industrial development also made it ideal for major participation in the war effort. Ontario was home to two major flight training centers—a P-38 training base stationed at the Municipal Airport and Cal-Aero in the South Ontario/Chino area.

Until 1941 the Ontario airport had only dirt runways. The year before, efforts were begun to upgrade the facility. Primary to the plans were the WPA-sanctioned funds to build a modern runway system. When completed, the facility had an east-west runway 6,200 feet long and a diagonal northeast-southwest runway 4,750 feet long.

By December 1942, with expansion construction underway, Arthur C. Nelson's Flying Service had 22 planes based at the single hangar where civilian flight instruction took place under the Federal Civil Pilot Training Program. And by December 1943 the expanded airport was dedicated as an Army Air Force P-38 Operational Training Base.

On June 15, 1940, at what is now known as Chino Airport, the Air Corps began building an air field, hangars, and barracks to train the thousands of pilots a war effort would require. By August 5 the first cadets were on hand to begin training. The facility was formally dedicated on September 14, 1940. During the intervening 40 days of frenetic building activity, a mile of sewers was put in, a sewage disposal plant was built, a complete water system with two wells and more than a mile of mains was installed, and a complete set of gas mains

and an underground electrical system were put in. Ten buildings containing concrete floors, central heating, and insulation were built. Roads, paved runways, a control tower, and a gasoline dispensing center were also part of the package. The mess hall could feed 600 cadets at once, and officers had their own mess.

The Cal-Aero flight school was a tremendous boost for Ontario's economy. More than 10,000 pilots graduated from the program. The greater part of the pilots' and the staff's pay found its way into the local economy.

World War II
On December 7, 1941, the Japanese bombed Pearl Harbor, and among the thousands killed in the attack were Joe and Don Lakin. Taking the loss personally, Ontario plunged into the war effort. The city, along with the rest of Southern California, immediately began to practice blackouts, and all major social events were cancelled, including Pasadena's Rose Parade.

The Red Cross moved into the old post office and Ontario women spent thousands of hours there making clothing and other necessary articles. A USO headquarters was set up at the Woman's Club in 1942, but in 1943 was moved to the Frankish Building. Citizens launched drives to sell Defense Bonds and the government urged local farmers to produce as much beef, pork, poultry, rabbits, and dairy products as they could. Victory gardens appeared for the first time since World War I. Everyone saved grease, foil, empty toothpaste tubes, paper, and rubber to be recycled, and peach growers provided pits for gas mask charcoal.

War Price and Rationing Boards regulated the dispersal of everyday items such as sugar, butter, shoes, meat, and coffee. Cigarettes became popular barter items, and gasoline was hoarded. Women went to work in the manufacturing plants, and everyone who could helped gather crops.

Exchange Orange Products produced a variety of products including juice concentrate, pectin, and dried orange meal for cattle feed. During World War II it was the largest citrus processing plant in California, employing 400 workers. Now under the ownership of Sunkist, the plant is still a major employer in Ontario. Courtesy, Ontario City Library, Model Colony History Room

The Ford Lunch, at the southeast corner of Holt Boulevard and Euclid Avenue, was started in 1912 by the Hobart brothers and supposedly named after their Model T. It became a nationally known landmark and was patronized by celebrities such as Douglas Fairbanks, Mary Pickford, Clark Gable, and Bob Hope. Many travelers stopped there on their way to Palm Springs. Courtesy, Ontario City Library, Model Colony History Room

In May 1942 Japanese residents of Ontario and Upland were among the 110,000 West Coast Japanese-Americans who were placed in internment camps. Many of the internees from Ontario and Upland were part of families that had settled in the area as early as 1900. The first stop for local internees was the Pomona Fair Grounds, which was converted to a temporary detention camp. But despite the harsh and unfair treatment, many young men from the Japanese community enlisted in the army, where they served in a segregated Japanese-American battalion that fought valiantly in the European theater of the war.

Women played a significant part in the war effort on all levels. Many entered the armed services. Businesswoman and Chaffey High School graduate Genevera Faye McQuatters enlisted in the WAACs (Women's Army Auxiliary Corps) in 1942. By the end of the war she had been commissioned as a major and was made assistant director of the WAAC Service Command. Many other women took civilian jobs in war plants while their children attended government-paid child care centers.

Local industry was also inducted into the war effort. The General Electric plant (formerly Hotpoint) began producing war goods such as socket wrench sets for trucks and other vehicles, oxygen pressure devices for aircraft, and containers used for dropping supplies and bombs by parachute. Exchange Orange Products prepared food products and juice concentrates for the troops. One Ontario man said he was served the juice in New Guinea. Kaiser Steel dedicated the blast furnace "Bess" in 1942 and began producing vehicle components and other steel products used in the war.

Ontario residents worked, sacrificed, and followed the war's progress both in Europe and in the Pacific as the United States crippled the Japanese fleet at Midway, the Allies invaded North Africa and Italy, and finally as the Allied troops stormed the Normandy beaches. On May 7, 1945, Germany surrendered. But the war in the Pacific raged on. With the rest of the world, Ontario gasped when atomic bombs were used on Japan in August, leading to Japan's surrender on August 15.

With the end of the war Ontario was changed forever. California had ceased to be an insulated entity in both the United States and the world. Ontario was now an aware member of the Pacific Rim, gaining direction for economic development over the next four decades.

The California Air National Guard's 163rd Fighter Group came to Ontario International Airport in the early 1950s. The airport's three north runway extensions, completed in 1952, 1956, and 1962, were financed by the ANG to accommodate their F-86 Sabrejets. Courtesy, Ontario City Library, Model Colony History Room

Growth and Rejuvenation

As early as 1905 the potential for Ontario to become a commuter city, particularly for Los Angeles jobs, was considered by grower and packing house manager C.D. Adams:

. . . 38 miles from Los Angeles, with which we are in the process of connection by electric railways, it is only a matter of time when we shall see our orange groves used as out of town homes by Los Angeles businessmen, who can do business there but live here in the dry and bracing atmosphere and step from their homes into the car and back again to their offices.

Adams' prediction was to come true during Ontario's postwar boom. Soon after World War II ended, men who had been stationed in California, and especially around Ontario, flooded back into the area, bringing families and a demand for housing. In 1946, 743 new homes were built in Ontario.

Furthermore, jobs were available. During the war, hundreds of millions of dollars had been poured into industrial development in California to create 5,000 new manufacturing plants. Women left their wartime jobs, leaving openings for the returning veterans.

In 1940, just prior to the war, Ontario's population had been 14,917. The 1946 count put the population at 19,638. By 1950 it was 22,872, and in the next 10 years the population more than doubled to 46,627. To accommodate this burgeoning population, groves and vineyards gave way to a new community phenomenon, the subdivision. And while many new residents found work locally, many others began commuting to jobs as far away as Los Angeles.

Wanting to cash in on the postwar boom in Southern California, Ontario's Chamber of Commerce redoubled its efforts to recruit business and industry. In 1947 the boast was that Ontario was "The Heart of Southern California."

The growth affected all of the city's social systems. Medical facilities at Upland's small Green's Memorial Hospital and the much larger San Antonio Community Hospital, both of which served Ontario, were being stretched to the limit, as were the area's schools, police, fire, and social services.

With the advent of the Korean War in 1950, most building was restricted with the exception of the new hospital to replace the hopelessly inadequate old Memorial Hospital.

The 224th Infantry Regiment of the California National Guard, 40th Division, temporarily located on the Chaffey College campus until a new armory was completed at John Galvin Park, and began recruiting for an additional 600 enlisted men and officers. The regiment departed on September 5, 1950. Everyone at home began to prepare for a possible atomic bomb attack.

When the conflict ended in 1953, Ontario once again felt the influx of veterans. It was returning veterans using the GI education bill who contributed to the increased enrollment in both Chaffey College adult school and daytime classes.

ABOVE: The Salvation Army occupied this building at the northwest corner of Euclid Avenue and Emporia Street from 1931 to 1972. The building was constructed to meet the needs of homeless men coming through Ontario during the Depression. Courtesy, Ontario City Library, Model Colony History Room

RIGHT: By 1886 there were enough Civil War veterans in Ontario and Cucamonga to form a Grand Army of the Republic Post. Ontario Post 124 of the G.A.R. was officially mustered on May 29 and the charter was dated July 2, 1886. Alois Podrasnik, top left, was a native of Czechoslovakia who fought as a first lieutenant in the war and later made his home in Upland. This photo was taken in April 1931. Courtesy, Ontario City Library, Model Colony History Room

than 70 churches and one synagogue existed in Ontario in 1960), city improvement groups, hospital auxiliary groups, and senior citizen's groups. In addition there were such organizations as those for political parties, AAUW (the American Association of University Women), PTA, West End Community Forum, National Conference of Christians and Jews, and the League of Women Voters of West San Bernardino County.

Fraternal groups, some of which were formed in the early years of the Colony, abounded, including the Elks, Eagles, and Masonic lodges, the American Legion, Veterans of Foreign Wars, Panhellenic (an organization of former collegiate sorority women), Daughters of the American Revolution, Disabled American Veterans, Daughters of the Golden West, Sons of Italy, Soroptimist International of Ontario, the Eastern Star, the Knights of Columbus, and the Independent Order of Odd Fellows (IOOF).

Ontario has also been home to numerous helping groups over the years including the House of Ruth for women who have been battered, Project Sister for rape survivors, and several 12-step rehabilitation programs including Al-Anon, Alcoholics Anonymous, and Narcotics Anonymous.

Ontario had grown enough to warrant a branch office of the County Department of Public Welfare. Many local residents have been helped over the years through such programs as old age security, aid to families with dependent children, aid to the totally disabled, and various kinds of medical assistance. Additional services have been added as the need is realized.

Medical Facilities

Public health also became a more complex issue as the population grew; so much so that the old Board of Health became inactive, bowing to the better organized and

The Ontario Rotary Club was founded October 2, 1922, by a group of 25 local businessmen. The club's first president was the Daily Report *publisher, Crombie Allen. In its early days the group met at the Casa Blanca Hotel on West Emporia Street. This photo shows a Rotary gathering on March 7, 1929. Courtesy, Ontario City Library, Model Colony History Room*

Plans for Ontario's public library date back to 1885 when a group of interested residents gathered at the Ontario Hotel for a "literary social." The library itself was housed in different locations until this building was constructed in 1906 with funding from philanthropist Andrew Carnegie. The building stood at the southwest corner of D Street and Euclid Avenue until its demolition in 1959. Courtesy, Ontario City Library, Model Colony History Room

financed County Health Department. In the 1960s health department programs operating in Ontario included the well baby clinic, the Oral Health Council, an orthopedic clinic plus the cerebral palsy and orthopedic clinic at Cypress, immunization clinics, tuberculosis clinics, several mobile x-ray units, postnatal and prenatal clinics, and the Mary Louise Griffith Heart Clinic at San Antonio Community Hospital.

There were also a school health program, public health nursing, and a full-blown sanitation department responsible for water purity, meat and dairy product safety, rodent and pest control, restaurant inspection, rubbish collection, public and private swimming pool inspection, school cafeterias, convalescent and foster home inspections, and sewage disposal.

In 1949 the Chamber of Commerce noted that two hospitals served the area—Green Memorial and San Antonio Community—with a total capacity of 106 beds. The roster of health professionals included 27 physicians, 6 chiropractors, 5 osteopaths, 1 chiropodist, 10 dentists, and 4 optometrists.

In 1951 Ontario Community Hospital replaced the old Memorial Hospital. On April 30 the first baby was born there. Over the next four decades both community hospitals would expand, with Ontario Community alone totalling 99 beds and a medical staff of more than 175 area-wide physicians. San Antonio Community Hospital expanded in 1963 to 128 beds. In the 1960s an expansion program added more than 180 new beds, and the hospital's size remained stable at 309 beds from 1973 through 1989.

Existing facilities were also brought up-to-date over the years. Radiology and nuclear medicine were added. Industrial medicine, addiction treatment centers, cardiopulmonary and respiratory treatment facilities, trauma centers, neonatal intensive care, physical therapy, and mental health services are among the medical capabilities of modern Ontario hospitals and clinics.

To accommodate growth and reflect changing needs of labor over the years, Ontario has gained the West End Industrial Medical Clinic, the Ontario Industrial Medical Clinic, the Hente Medical Clinic, the Ontario Community Medical Clinic, and the Ontario Community Medical Center.

Cultural Development

Since George Chaffey's plans to attract educated families to his colony, cultural activities have played an important part in the city's development.

The first library was a volunteer effort and the first librarian, Alfred Piddington, a volunteer. It was started in November 1885 with a meeting at the Ontario Hotel. A reading room was set up at the hotel, with assets of 220 books and $40 cash. In subsequent years the library location shifted from place to place. Thanks to an endowment by Andrew Carnegie, however, Ontario was able to build a permanent library in 1906. When the Carnegie library was unable to meet earthquake standards, the building was razed in 1959 and a new library was dedicated on Lemon and C streets, its present location, in 1961. Additions to the library continue. By its centennial in 1985, the library offered the public access to 214,000 books and publications, as well as films, records, cassettes, periodicals, newspapers, and videotapes.

Over the years the community has

Ontario's first radio station, KOCS-AM, began broadcasting on January 26, 1947. The studio was housed in the Daily Report *building on B Street next to the newspaper offices. Jerene Appleby Harnish, owner of the paper, is shown here accepting an award from the Veterans of Foreign Wars. Courtesy, Ontario City Library, Model Colony History Room*

The Union Pacific Railway came to Ontario in 1903. The station was located just east of Euclid Avenue on the north side of the tracks near State Street. The building, built in the Mission Revival style, was demolished in 1976 after the Union Pacific discontinued freight operations at the station. Photo by Claude L. Wilson. Courtesy, Wilson's Photo Supplies

enjoyed a rich cultural life through the Chaffey Community Art Association and arts festivals, the Garrick Players, the West End Symphony, and the West End Opera Association, organized in 1965. One of the highlights for all Ontario residents was the national premiere of Ontarian and former Chaffey music department head, S. Earle Blakeslee's opera *Red Cloud* in 1970. Blakeslee's fascination with Native American legends dated back to the early 1920s. An early opera of his, the *Legend of Wiwaste,* was first presented in Ontario in 1924 and excerpts were performed in 1927 at the Hollywood Bowl as part of inter-tribal Indian ceremonies. In the past the Civic Concert Association staged concerts featuring top musical artists at Spring Auditorium. The old Foothill Music and Drama Association presented light opera and drama.

The 2,500-seat Gardiner Spring Auditorium, larger than Los Angeles' Ahmanson and slightly smaller than Claremont's Bridges, also continues to be a focal point for cultural activities, and has offered such fare over the years as plays, operas, musicals, and lectures. Among the artists and troupes to perform there are Metropolitan Opera star Helen Traubel, violinist Yehudi Menuhin, and the Ballet Russe, as well as pianist Jose Iturbi, the Boston Pops, actors Marlene Dietrich, Jimmy Durante, and George Raft, and orchestra leader Xavier Cugat.

Ontario's Gallery Theater, a theater-in-the-round that seats 200, has offered the community a variety of comedies, musicals, and plays over the years.

Redevelopment and Historical Preservation

By the 1970s some areas of Ontario were showing wear and tear. In November 1971 Ontario joined a host of other cities taking advantage of the 1963 California Community Redevelopment law. Areas chosen for redevelopment were eligible for special financing. Projects chosen included the 1978 Ontario Vintage Industrial Park, 3,500 acres on the east side of the city. Several major corporations have taken advantage of the benefits offered by locating in a redevelopment project area. Among those who have developed or are planning to develop distribution centers are K mart Corporation, Mervyn's Department Stores, the Chrysler Corporation, Jerseymaid, Fruit Growers Supply Company, and Inland Container. These projects brought in 2,000 new jobs.

As Ontario approached the centennial of its founding, the community became increasingly concerned about retaining its historical buildings. One preservation effort was creating new uses for the historical city government buildings, many of which were built in the 1930s in the Mission Revival style favored by so many WPA projects. A newly established Museum of History and Art was located in the old city hall building. The Gardiner Spring Auditorium was also slated for restoration.

Between 1883 and 1908 three fountains were placed on Euclid Avenue. The first was built by George Chaffey to advertise the colony's water supply. For years a depression marked the location of George Chaffey's ground-level fountain on Euclid near the Southern Pacific tracks. Though the fountain still existed, it had become buried by soil build-up over the years. It was rediscovered during excavation of the site when the Euclid Avenue underpass was built. Broken pieces of the Chaffey fountain were donated to the Museum of History and Art.

Charles Frankish designed and built the second fountain. Refurbished in 1952 and meticulously maintained since, it still stands in front of the old city hall building. The third fountain was built by the Women's Christian Temperance Union and located on the sidewalk in front of the Citizens Bank. That fountain has had several homes and several

ABOVE: This photo of Ontario International Airport in 1952 shows Lockheed, Douglas, and Northrop aircraft, including the last Northrop Flying Wing (upper right) shortly before it was destroyed by order of the United States Government. Courtesy, Ontario City Library, Model Colony History Room

LEFT: The 1960s brought jet traffic to Ontario when the airport was designated an alternate landing site for Los Angeles International Airport. These passengers found themselves in Ontario sunshine as opposed to Los Angeles fog in December 1961. Courtesy, Ontario City Library, Model Colony History Room

The first California 500 race was held at the Ontario Motor Speedway on September 6, 1970. The second race, shown here, was run on September 3, 1971. The raceway continued to operate for 10 years until financial problems forced its closure and sale to the Chevron Land and Development Company in late 1980. Courtesy, Ontario City Library, Model Colony History Room

refurbishings. The latest fixing and relocation occurred in 1975 when the Kiwanis Club retrieved it from the John Galvin Park. It is now on Euclid between Holt and B streets.

C.C. "Kip" and Elinore Carlson, to honor their son Donald's memory, galvanized friends and relatives to restore the old mule car. Donald Carlson, a city employee who died of a rare blood disorder, had a personal dream of restoring the mule car replica, which had been built for the city's diamond jubilee in 1957. Carlson had seen the replica mule car stored at the city maintenance yard. The car and a specially sculpted mule are housed on Euclid Avenue in a building donated by the Carlsons.

The Ontario Historic Landmarks Society, formed as a nonprofit organization in 1975, is a central mover in retaining Ontario's past and works closely with the Ontario Library's historical archives staff in the Model Colony History Room. The Historic Landmarks Society identifies and encourages restoration of historic buildings and sites in Ontario.

Communication

Ontario was one of the first cities in the country to have a studio that could broadcast in the new FM frequency. At 2:40 p.m. on Novemebr 23, 1945, the owners of the *Daily Report* received a telegram from the Federal Communications Commission giving permission to operate a community FM radio station.

Thousands of residents attended Ontario's first FM radio broadcast on January 26, 1947, at the Chaffey Auditorium. Celebrities Barbara Hale, Bill Williams, and Alan Young were on hand, and actor Pat O'Brien was master of ceremonies. The station, KOCS AM and KEDO FM, was located in the new two-story *Daily Report* building. In 1989 Ontario's radio needs were being met by a number of out-of-area stations. KNTF maintained a Post Office Box for patrons in Ontario, but was broadcast out of Rancho Cucamonga.

The *Daily Report*, Ontario's major newspaper since 1910, was privately owned until 1965, when Jerene Appleby Harnish retired from publishing and sold the paper

The Ontario Plaza, at Mountain Avenue and 4th Street, is a good example of the neighborhood shopping centers built in the late 1950s and early 1960s to serve the rapidly expanding residential areas in Ontario. Most of the shopping centers and housing tracts were built on former grove land. Courtesy, Ontario City Library, Model Colony History Room

to T.A. Richardson, owner of the *Pomona Progress Bulletin*. Two years later Richardson sold all of his holdings to Donrey Media. As part of an ongoing consolidation and expansion program, Donrey moved the *Daily Report* into a new building on Fourth Street on October 13, 1987. In September 1989 the historic building on B Street was demolished.

The Ontario area has been served by television broadcast stations from Los Angeles since the 1940s. Local viewers have been able to tune in to a rich variety of information and entertainment over the years as broadcasting capabilities expanded the number of channels available.

Satellite communications broadened the information base and increased the speed with which Ontarians could be informed. In the 1970s a new communications capability came to Ontario via cable. Since George Chaffey developed the first long distance telephone line, Ontario had never lacked the latest communications innovations. This vision continues today with residents being able to attend city council meetings from the comfort of their homes via Comcast Cable Company on Channel 3.

Transportation Comes of Age

The 1957 Chamber of Commerce motto was "Ideally Situated." Ontario was served by three railroads: Southern Pacific, Union Pacific, and Santa Fe; Ontario International Airport; the newly constructed San Bernardino Freeway, California State Highway 71, and U.S. highways 60, 66, 70, and 99. Los Angeles was a blissful and accessible 40 minutes away by car and one hour by truck during rush hour.

Four transcontinental bus lines also converged on the area, not to mention the fact that Metropolitan Coach bus line had announced service to San Bernardino and Los Angeles. Several trucking companies, both local and long-distance, also operated in the area.

By the end of World War II the airport had become the hub of transportation and the center around which most new industrial developments were clustered. In 1946 the airport designation changed from municipal to international with the addition of Pacific Overseas Airlines' DC-3 cargo flights. The first direct delivery of airmail was made to Ontario International Airport (OIA) in June 1951. By 1953 the airport, with its two runways and modern control tower with an instrument landing system, was about to enter the jet age.

Aircraft industries at or adjacent to the airport became major employers. Lockheed Aircraft Service set up shop in 1952. Two years later General Electric Aircraft Apparatus Service Shop started operations. In addition, Douglas and Northrop had facilities located at OIA. The 196th Fighter Group of the California Air National Guard located at Ontario's airport in 1952. The group was renamed the 163rd Fighter Group in 1958, following a reorganization and expansion of the California Air National Guard. Along with the fighter group came an instrument landing system, and a runway extension to handle the Guard's F86 Sabrejets.

By 1960 the airport was handling 23,000 passengers a year and a passenger terminal was finally completed with part of the $2 million Airport Revenue Bond approved by the voters 6 to 1 in 1956. After the Federal Aviation Administration designated OIA as a provisional alternate to Los Angeles International Airport in 1967, negotiations between Los Angeles and Ontario led to a joint powers agreement to give operational control of the airport to the Los Angeles Department of Airports.

PSA began the first regular jet service from OIA in 1968. Air Cal and Continental followed, and in the 1970s United Airlines and American Airlines started service. In February 1973 Ontario International Airport was the first Southern California

Prior to 1950 much of Ontario was still covered with orange groves, as this photo of Mountain Avenue shows. Bellevue cemetery is seen in the center of the photo on the west side of the street. Courtesy, Ontario City Library, Model Colony History Room

airport to receive an official certification of operation from the FAA. In 1981 a 10,200-foot runway was added to accommodate wide-body aircraft.

Between 1967 and 1984 nearly $20 million in capital improvements were made at the airport. Air carrier service expanded to 14 airlines handling more than 2 million passengers and 112 million pounds of air cargo per year.

Changing Face of the City

As the suburbs spread out and away from Ontario's core, commuters and busy homemakers welcomed a new social and economic experiment—the shopping center or plaza. These new centers-away-from-the-center were so popular that longtime downtown merchants and businesses suffered severely. Downtowns all across the nation began to become less important, and Ontario did not escape that fate.

Neighborhood shopping centers sprang up in the 1960s where the new housing was going in. In the Ontario area centers were built along Mountain and Holt, in the Monte Vista area (later renamed Montclair when it achieved cityhood), in the southern part of the city along Euclid, and to the east along Fourth. Some of the city's oldest businesses either relocated or opened up satellite stores. All this activity served to drain business and traffic away from Ontario's traditional downtown.

To make matters worse for Southern California downtowns, huge regional shopping centers were built. One of the largest, the Montclair Plaza, was completed in 1968. It would take nearly 20 years for downtowns to come up with formulas to draw people back. Ironically, the very growth that contributed to the fragmentation of cities is now contributing to their rejuvenation. Increasing traffic, while a great frustration for commuters, is keeping shoppers closer to home.

After investing nearly $500,000 in downtown renewal studies, in 1989 Ontario

was still contemplating the advantages of the Main Street program developed by the National Trust for Historic Preservation, which was a proven success in 130 other cities nationwide.

Ontario Motor Speedway

Construction of the $25.5-million Ontario Motor Speedway (OMS), built on 700 acres at Haven and the San Bernardino Freeway, marked a colorful period in Ontario history. It was to rival the Indianapolis Motor Speedway. The grandstand seating capacity was 85,000, and the winner's circle was made of bricks from the old Indianapolis brickyard. During its 10-year history racing greats such as Mario Andretti, Graham Hill, Mark Donahue, and daredevil Evel Knieval made appearances on the track.

In 1971, 1974, and 1978 thousands of fans flocked to OMS for major rock concerts. The speedway struggled financially and finally gave up, selling its property to Chevron Land and Development Company. The grandstand and raceways were razed to make way for construction of the Ontario International Center. The winner's circle bricks were saved, however, and removed to the basement of the Museum of History and Art.

Citrus and Vines Give Way to Housing and Industry

In 1948, 2,000 acres of citrus grew in the city, and there were an additional 18,000 acres within the city's sphere of influence. Other crops included walnuts, peaches, hay, beans, sweet potatoes, and olives. Also within the confines of the city were dairy ranches, poultry ranches, and even rabbit growers. Income from citrus and other agricultural products provided a high level of income for the area.

But a cold snap in January 1949 was to be the beginning of the end for citrus. In the preceding years hundreds of acres had been sold and developed into housing

San Secondo d'Asti Catholic Church is part of a patriarchal colony built by Secondo Guasti. In addition to the church, the colony had a school and a farm operation large enough to support Guasti's family and the workers at his company's vineyards. Photo by Bo Richards

ABOVE: San Secondo d'Asti Catholic Church served as the religious center of the company town of Guasti. The town housed the workers of the Italian Vineyard Company. Photo by Bo Richards

RIGHT: By the end of World War II, Ontario offered a near complete blend of cultural, educational, religious, and social opportunities. Pictured here is St. George's Catholic Church. Photo by Bo Richards

ABOVE: In 1900 Italian immigrant Secondo Guasti realized his dream when he purchased 4,000 acres of land and began planting a vineyard. This became the foundation of Guasti's Italian Vineyard Company. Photo by Bo Richards

LEFT: The holding tanks at Secondo Guasti's Italian Vineyard Company housed 5 million gallons of wine at the height of the firm's operations. The company's buildings are located at the edge of Ontario International Airport. Photo by Bo Richards

ABOVE: These strawberry fields reflect Ontario's heritage as an agricultural community. The area's ideal climate, coupled with aggressive, experimental efforts by local growers, enabled Ontario to more than fulfill its destiny as envisioned by city founder George B. Chaffey, Jr. Photo by Bob Reyburn

LEFT: Ontario International Airport is a full-service origin and destination airport with commercial jet service to every major city in the United States, as well as to many international destinations. OIA also serves as a major air-freight hub for various freight companies, including United Parcel Service and Federal Express. Photo by John Gale

The availability of affordable housing, excellent health care facilities, good schools and nearby colleges, and a growing reputation as a cultural center enable Ontario to maintain its reputation as an excellent place to live and raise a family. Photo by John Gale

ABOVE: Older residences, lovingly restored and maintained, can be found throughout Ontario's neighborhoods. Shown here is the old Bradford House, located at 813 Euclid Avenue. Photo by Bo Richards

LEFT: Ontario is combining its propensity for forward thinking with a deep regard for the preservation of its roots. Part of the city's downtown redevelopment project includes a park on Central Parkway and Euclid Avenue which includes an historic exhibit on Ontario's early railroad as well as this water fountain erected in 1908 by the Womens' Christian Temperance Union. Photo by Bo Richards

Ontario International Airport is one of the 100 busiest airports in the world. In 1988 it served 4.7 million passengers; that figure is expected to reach 12 million by the year 2000. Photo by Bo Richards

tracts. Groves and homes were in close proximity. On January 4 temperatures dropped as low as 20 degrees. Farmers lit smudge pots the night before and kept them burning until daylight, and the freeze lasted into the next day.

Economically, it was a disaster. Each smudge pot cost $4 per hour to burn. In spite of the extensive smudging efforts, crop losses by the next day were estimated at $8 to $10 million.

It was also a disaster politically. New residents protested loudly against the smudging. The atmosphere was so thick from the malodorous smoke that school buses were late. Farmers and old-timers maintained the murk was much better than previous years—because the new heaters burned more efficiently and they no longer burned tires. In fact, it was nothing compared with the 1937 three-week freeze during which smudging led to severe burn accidents that resulted in two deaths and seven injuries. During the winter of 1937 schools were shut down completely because of low visibility. Nevertheless, the controversy and outrage over the 1949 smudging, faction against faction, lasted more than a year.

One year after the freeze the Ontario City Council asked the County Board of Supervisors for a pledge of support in regulating the combustion of smudge pots in the city limits. After two months of vociferous meetings, the City Council passed an ordinance prohibiting smudging in residential and commercial zones in the city limits and setting a fee and permit system for smudging in the agricultural zones.

Perhaps not so coincidentally, 1949-1950 was the last season for the Ontario-Cucamonga Exchange Growers' packing plant. They closed their doors, sending the growers to other packers, and filed dissolution papers in 1951. As more and more groves were cut down, other packers followed suit.

Up through the 1940s local vineyards flourished. In 1948 total acreage exceeded 20,000. More than 20 wineries existed in and near Ontario. Unlike citrus, vestiges of the great vineyards and wine tradition were somewhat slower to go.

Perhaps the first and most significant bite out of the large vineyards and agricultural holdings occurred when Henry J. Kaiser built a steel mill in 1942, in Fontana, near the outskirts of Ontario's city limits. A second bite out of the vineyards was made by Ontario International Airport's expansion in the 1950s.

Careful planning and diligence on the part of the grape growers cooperative, Cucamonga Pioneer Vineyard Association (an outgrowth of the 1911 Cucamonga Vintage Co.), had kept local grape growers, winemakers, and vintners on an even keel. Growers and winemakers were able to change their product to meet the public's changing tastes from sweet dessert wines to drier table wines. As James Hofer notes in *Cucamonga Wines and Vines: A History of the Cucamonga Pioneer Vineyard Association*, the seeds of the vineyards' decline were planted in the sandy soil of the 1940s.

The largest winery, Garrett and Company's Virginia Dare Winery at Haven and Foothill, started to decline after the death of Cap'n Garrett in 1940. Though the winery reached its peak in 1943 when it began touting itself as the world's largest vineyard, it was merely moving on the momentum established by Garrett.

By the 1950s the Garrett family could no longer hold the corporate structure together. They sold 571 acres to an investment company and leased the winery to Alta Vineyards and later to the Wine Growers Guild who, in 1959, changed the name to Guild Wine Co. In 1961 the winery built 50 years earlier by George Chaffey's viticulturist, John Klusman, was liquidated and sold. Three years later, fire gutted the buildings.

However, the main Guasti holdings

The Mission Winery was established in 1911 by John Klusman, a German immigrant, and Colonel M.E. Post, a land speculator. In 1918 the winery was sold to Garrett and Company who had been leasing the buildings and land since 1912. Garrett renamed the winery Virginia Dare. Courtesy, Tower Partnership, Rancho Cucamonga

on 11 acres along Guasti Road next to the Ontario International Airport were purchased by Philo Biane in 1957. Biane, who had been manager of the vineyards and winery at Guasti for Garrett and Company and later for Guild Wineries, leased an additional set of buildings on the site. One of Biane's ancestors, Theophile Vache, was a member of one of France's oldest winemaking families who came to California during the period when Mexico was ruled by the Napoleons. Biane revived the Brookside name for a winery his family had owned in San Timoteo Canyon near Redlands, and developed a highly successful direct-to-the-public operation with tasting rooms in several cities.

But eventually Biane retired to a small vineyard above Alta Loma and sold Brookside to Beatrice Foods. The energy was gone from the winery, and Beatrice eventually sold to a group more interested in the location next door to the airport than in wine production.

According to Hofer the decline of the wineries can be attributed to the decline in the number of acres planted in grapes. In 1960, 23,000 acres were planted

in vines, but by 1968 acreage was down to 16,000.

Sometime in the early 1970s those left in the business gave up hope. Hofer says no one expected the industry to last out the twentieth century. By 1969 many growers, Biane included, were planting vineyards in Temecula and Rancho California. Many things conspired against the quality of the harvest and, therefore, the quality of wine, including a water table lowered by domestic and industrial usage, air pollution, changing labor laws and patterns, and tax rates that favored industrial rather than agricultural use of the land.

In 1989 there were still a few diehards hanging on to the tradition and they maintained that the area could still grow the kinds of grapes, Mission and Palomino, needed for sweet wines. Biane was producing limited quantities of Triple Cream Sherry, and though not in the Ontario city limits, nearby Filippi, San Antonio, and Galleano, after nearly 50 years, were still in operation.

The 1980s saw the demise of the state's oldest winery, Thomas Winery. Though the building was preserved as a historical monument, winery operations faded away. At one time in the 1980s, the Filippi family purchased the old winery, but later sold it. The Thomas label continues as Filippi Vintage Co., however, producing a product sold as Thomas Wine in the Guasti retail store.

Agriculture in the form of dairy farming was holding out on the southern outskirts of Ontario as a 14,000 acre agricultural preserve. Its existence is guaranteed until 1997.

With the 1989 study that detected contaminants in the ground water as the result of the presence of the dairy herds, the future of the preserve is in even greater doubt. It seems clear that by the turn of the century agriculture will be a memory in the valley, with the preferred use of the land being light industry and housing.

Commanding a view of the San Gabriel Mountains, this six-story building is part of CentreLake Plaza, a 70-acre mixed-use master-planned business park currently under development near the Ontario International Airport and the I-10 freeway. The park will house offices, retail shops, hotels, and restaurants, and the grounds will be carefully landscaped with winding pedestrian paths and two artificial lakes. Photo by Michael J. Elderman

BMW of North America opened their 207,000-square-foot parts distribution center on Milliken Avenue in the California Commerce Center in 1987. Because of an existing foreign trade zone, BMW can import parts to Ontario without paying import duties until the items are shipped out of the zone. Photo by Michael J. Elderman

Where the Future Takes Flight

A September 1989 *San Bernardino County Sun* article stated that back in 1972 a prominent developer took one look at the Ontario-Cucamonga plain with its acres of grape vines and saw a sea of green. "It was the color of money," said writers Theresa Walker and Tony Saavedra.

Resources that developer Ted Dutton saw were the same ones the Ontario Chamber of Commerce had been touting since 1942: an international airport dedicated to keeping up with growth, two major freeways, three rail lines, and lots of developable land.

The seeds of the rapid industrial expansion of the 1980s were planted in the 1950s. As a transportation hub with thousands of acres of land available for commercial and industrial use, it was a logical economic move on the part of the city and the Chamber of Commerce to smooth the way for industrial growth.

In the 1950s Ontario began plans to develop and zone areas specifically for commerce. In the late 1950s the city designated 2,000 acres of unoccupied land south of the airport for the Ontario Industrial Park, east of Campus Avenue between Mission and the Pomona Freeway. By 1961 the Industrial Park was a reality.

Chamber of Commerce publications spanning the last 40 years dramatically reflect the economic changes. Agriculture interests dominated the 1949 publication. Industry and manufacturing, while far from token, were nevertheless secondary. Thirteen years later the *Daily Report*'s promotional brochure boasted that Ontario, with its several major employers and host of smaller manufacturers in combination with historic citrus and wine grape production, provided the area with a balanced, stable, and self-contained economy.

That year, 1962, Ontario boasted 102 manufacturing plants. Major items being produced included irons and other electric appliances, citrus products, pharmaceuticals, clothing, building materials, trailers, and aircraft servicing. The largest employers were Lockheed, General Electric (originally Hotpoint), Exchange Orange Products, General Electric Co.'s jet engine plant, Fruehauf Trailers, and Bestile Mfg. All were keeping company with large, if not entirely healthy, agricultural businesses.

In contrast, nearly 30 years later the 1989 Chamber publication makes absolutely no mention of agriculture and touts a tremendous growth in commercial and industrial land-use. The Chamber's roster listed more than 1,000 members in a broad variety of professional, manufacturing, commercial, and service industry related categories. In the 1980s the Model Colony's beginnings as a fruit and citrus community became history.

Bernice Bedford Conley, in *Dreamers and Dwellers*, quotes a 1981 statement by the state secretary of the California Citrus Producers Association saying that citrus returns had been going down steadily since 1945 and in 1981 were below the cost of production. According to Conley, in 1981 "Agriculture had almost completely disappeared from the economy, and fruit orchards and citrus groves were no more within the city limits."

Sometime in the early 1980s the last grove within Ontario's city limits was cut down. Many groves were removed by their owners in anticipation of future building, but perhaps the most compelling reason had to do with poor economic returns. A great deal of citrus acreage was turned into strawberry fields, a holding action by the owners that allowed the land to be in use and provide some sort of profit margin.

In an October 1989 interview, Rick Starratt, a son-in-law of the Latimer family who own San Antonio Orchards packing, said the Latimer family moved its packing plant to Riverside around 1982. The bookkeeping and accounting headquarters remain in Ontario, however, "for sentimental reasons." Ontario's first airport, Latimer Field, was named for Charles Latimer's packinghouse.

While Ontario grew no commercial citrus of its own in 1989, there were two major citrus-based businesses in Ontario—Dole Citrus and Sunkist Growers, Inc./Ontario Orange Products Division.

Dole Citrus' Administration and Sales Center is located in the Kline Center near the airport. The company specializes in growing, packing, and selling fresh citrus and has several major operations throughout the citrus growing sections of the United States. Dole Citrus chose its current location for two reasons: to gain proximity to the airport and to centralize the commute for employees when Dole Citrus' parent company, Castle & Cooke, acquired the recently consolidated Blue Goose packing of Fullerton and E.T. Wall of Riverside.

Sunkist Growers, Inc./Ontario Orange Products Division is one of the area's largest employers. The plant, which performs research to develop products from the juice, peel, and oil of oranges and lemons, is equipped for extraction, blending, evaporation, freezing, and pressing the citrus for use in more than 1,600

juice and peel products. Many of the products are manufactured there and include juice, juice concentrates, pectins, soft drink bases, pharmaceuticals, dry citrus flavors, and livestock feed.

Industry, manufacturing, and lifestyle were the attributes Ontario was touting during the 1980s to draw even more people and more business to the area. It was a natural draw because Ontario was ranked as the seventh-fastest growing city in California.

Ontario still had relatively low-cost land compared with Los Angeles and Orange counties. In 1985, to further boost industrial and commercial growth, the city negotiated for a large portion of the California Commerce Center's 1,855 acres to be included in the Port of Long Beach Foreign Trade Zone. In its first four years of existence more than a dozen companies moved to the California Commerce Center specifically to take advantage of the duty-free zone.

Besides the California Commerce Center, the Santa Fe-Southern Pacific Corporation owns several hundred acres in Ontario destined for development and resale. Other parks included the Vintage Industrial Park, Ontario Interchange Properties, and several distribution centers including K mart, Chrysler, Nordstrom, Miller's Outpost, and Mervyn's.

Commercial growth in Ontario is demonstrated by figures on taxable retail sales, which were $57.5 million in 1960 and $763 million in 1986. Ontario was eighth in the state in retail sales in 1984, and was expected to reach sixth place by 1990 with anticipated sales of $9.5 billion.

Among the additions being made in 1989 were several business parks including the Ontario Center being developed on the former Ontario Motor Speedway by Chevron Land and Development Company, the Kline Center, Transpark, Ontario International Place, Ontario Airport Center, Centrelake Business Park, and Koll

The Ontario Hilton Hotel is part of the Ontario Center, a 675-acre mixed use development in northeast Ontario built on the old Ontario Motor Speedway site. Courtesy, The Daily Report

Haven Business Center.

A host of hotels sprang up to accommodate travelers and business people, and along with them a burgeoning convention and conference industry. Besides the Clarion, Red Lion Inns have located near the airport, as have the Ontario Airport Hilton, Best Western Ontario Airport, Holiday Inn-Ontario International Airport, Lexington Hotel Suites, and the Quality Inn Hotel.

Ontario's place of importance in the rapidly growing Inland Empire and on the Pacific Rim has been tempered by some very real social and environmental challenges. Though some problems are local in nature, most are shared with other cities in Southern California and are of regional concern. Among these are air pollution, airport noise, waste disposal, and congestion on freeways, highways, roads, and streets. More than 7,700 homes are located in the airport's path, and the three-year airport noise study completed in 1989 concluded

that the jet noise was great enough for the city to receive federal aid to soundproof schools and homes in the flight path, and that flights needed to be steered away from residential areas and jets needed to be fitted with quieter engines. City of Chino officials claimed that they were shut out of the study and that little or no relief for the city was offered in the report. Chino, at the end of 1989, was contesting the study results.

In her column in the June 1981 Ontario Historic Landmarks Society newsletter, Vicki Alexander recalled earlier noise problems with the airport:

In January of 1930, six Army planes used the local field for student flying practice. It seems the roar of the motors frightened local hens into an early grave. "They (the hens) flew about in a frenzy trying to escape the demons of the air, and when the ships had passed on, a check of the casualties revealed four hens in one pen suffer-

ing from broken wings." According to a news-paper article this necessitated the slaying and sub-sequent chicken dinner for the family. So take heart, the noise may keep you awake, it may inter-fere with your television, but unless you are a chicken it won't kill you.

Annexation issues are critical to Ontario, which in mid-1989 had only 400 acres left to use for housing developments. Competition is high among West End cities for annexations, spheres of influence, and just plain elbow room.

Hemmed in by Ontario's Creekside Village and the California Commerce Center, as well as subdivisions of East Chino, is the Chino Valley Agricultural Preserve. It is among the last large chunks of land potentially available to Ontario. But it belongs to neither Ontario nor Chino. The agricultural preserve lands are the center of controversy because both cities want to be able to annex the land when the 1997 moratorium expires.

Newspaper stories predict a major struggle between Chino and Ontario for the 14,000 acres. On them is housed the largest concentration of dairy cattle in the United States—more than 160,000 cows owned by 203 dairies. The preserve also shelters numerous poultry farms. The

preserve plays no mean part in Ontario's economy with an estimated product value of $347 million. In addition, many of the 1,000 milkers live in Ontario. Dairy- and poultry-related businesses in the area account for another 2,500 jobs.

As Ontario heads toward its centennial of incorporation in 1991 its economic future as a transportation and industrial hub for the Inland Empire seems assured. Over the years the airport that began as a small field near Latimer's packinghouse has served to attract business centers, industry, manufacturing, office space, warehousing, and a large hotel and service industry. Ontario International Airport provides a $3-billion economic nucleus for the Inland Empire.

As noted before, by 1989 Ontario was landlocked. A mere 400 acres remained for housing development, while the industrial lands were just beginning to be utilized. People had been moving into Ontario at the rate of 5,400 a year since 1980, and in 1989, as reflected in school enrollment, there seemed to be no sign of a slow-down. Along with this population boom, the faces in the community were undergoing a drastic change.

In 1989 Chaffey Union High School's students from minority backgrounds dominated the campus. Hispanic, Black, Asian, and students from the Pacific Islands increased in the largest numbers over a 10-year period from 1979 to 1989. But unlike other school districts that have seen increases in racial tensions, Ontario remained relatively peaceful as the campus ethnic mix changed.

As in all the cities in the county, crime statistics climbed. The drug problem has also plagued Ontario, and the city has joined other communities in the county to form anti-drug campaigns aimed at youth. Ontario also participated in the formation of the county-wide task force to combat gang activities.

One plus for families moving to the area is the location nearby of several four-

Creekside Village, a 410-acre residential project containing 2,600 units, opened in 1980. A planned community, it has two day-care centers, running tracks, and lakes that can be used for sailing and boating. Courtesy, The Daily Report

year colleges and universities. Among those are California Polytechnic University, Claremont College, Claremont Graduate School, Harvey Mudd College, Scripps College, Pitzer College, Pomona College, University of La Verne, and Southern California School of Theology. Just a little farther away there is California State University, San Bernardino; University of California, Riverside; and the University of Redlands.

Ontario's churches and social clubs and organizations provide a rich and well-rounded environment. More than 80 churches and synagogues are located in or near Ontario. In addition, the community has growing numbers of other religious groups living in its borders, including follow-ers of Buddhism, Islam, and Hinduism.

Social clubs and service organizations abound, with around 100 listed by the Chamber of Commerce in 1989. Reflecting a gradual change in social consciousness, a gay group was also listed in the Chamber publication.

Ontario's greatest asset has always been its civic-minded citizens, the people who have chosen to live in the shadow of the San Gabriel Mountains, within reach of the rest of the world. In 1989, two years before the former Model Colony's incorporation centennial, Ontario provided the area with a new kind of role model embodied in the name of a new street in its most modern area of development near the airport—Inland Empire Boulevard.

Ontario's first Independence Day parade took place in 1895. Like most of the town's businesses and social groups, the Ontario National Bank participated in the parade. The bank's entry in 1911 was this car, owned by cashier George McCrea. It was decorated with roses from Armstrong Nurseries. Seated in the car are some Chaffey High School students, including McCrea's two daughters. Courtesy, Ontario City Library, Model Colony History Room

Central Market was located on Euclid Avenue next to Jacob Jesson's Drug Store. A.J. Williams, the manager, is seen on the left, behind the counter. Courtesy, Ontario City Library, Model Colony History Room

Partners in Progress

What set Ontario apart from many other Southern California settlements started during the land boom of the late 1800s was the way it was created out of a carefully conceived and novel plan, not because a group of pioneers had stumbled upon it and decided the land looked like a good place to homestead. Nor because they had been lured from the East by dishonest land promoters touting benefits that were either greatly exaggerated or nonexistent—an all too common experience.

George Chaffey, a Canadian-born engineer, and his brother, William, had come to Riverside in 1880 with ambitious plans to establish model colonies. They started with an agricultural community near San Bernardino that they named Etiwanda, attracting settlers from the Midwest and Canada with, among other things, membership in a mutual water company that guaranteed adequate irrigation for each land parcel. So successful was the venture that in 1882 George Chaffey bought 6,000 acres of land to begin another one, calling it Ontario, after his native province in Canada.

He installed all basic improvements before any land was offered for sale, including streets properly laid out and, again, creation of a mutual water company, all of which sent a singular expression of trustworthiness to potential buyers. Retaining his rights for the use of the water to generate electricity, he even made plans to provide power for the colony's settlers, an idea that would be implemented in 1891 with the establishment of the San Antonio Electric Light and Power Company, giving Ontario claim to the first commercially successful hydroelectric plant in the West.

Chaffey's unique method of colonization was enormously successful, attracting wide attention everywhere, and soon those early settlers began the process that would transform Ontario into a prosperous citrus, olive, grape, and wine producer, a role that would be its economic mainstay for decades to come.

Today, however, the city is leaving its agricultural heritage behind as it becomes possibly the fastest-growing business and industrial community in the Inland Empire. Still offering reasonably priced land, it features an unbeatable combination of ready access to a network of major freeways and Ontario International Airport, a large pool of skilled and unskilled labor, affordable housing, and a supportive, forward-looking city government and administration. Once again, as in the late 1800s, Ontario has become a magnet attracting "Partners in Progress" who know a good thing when they see it.

The support of many of Ontario's businesses, industries, professions, and organizations, some of whose histories reach back into Ontario's beginnings and others whose histories are still being written, has made possible the publication of this book. Their stories are on the following pages.

ONTARIO CHAMBER OF COMMERCE

In 1909, 27 years after Ontario's founding in 1882, the local merchants' association decided that the time had come to organize a chamber of commerce to deal with the increasing business and community concerns of a city rapidly emerging from its fledgling pioneer days.

A committee was formed, consisting of E.D. Abrams, G.R. Holbrook, W.W. Smith, C.D. Van Wie, W.A. Freemire, E.H. Richardson, and H.E. Swan. The group first met in the Masonic Hall on October 7, 1909, and, a week later, on October 14, held an organizational meeting with C.G.H. Bennink as chairman and F.E. Unholz as secretary. It was attended by 100 Ontario residents, 78 of whom signed up as active members. Monthly dues were set at 50 cents.

Freemire, who later would become mayor of Ontario, was elected president of the new chamber of commerce. On October 21 he was joined by an elected board of directors that included several members of the original committee: Abrams, Smith, Van Wie, and Richardson, plus Dr. C.A. Warmer, Glenn D. Smith, J.B. Harvey, Abel Armstrong, C.F. Moore, G.N. Poe, and J.C. Morris.

In the following years the Ontario Chamber of Commerce would take an active leadership role in the development of the growing community, working on such crucial projects as schools, parks, protection of the city's water supply, and promoting the area nationwide. In 1916 it also introduced the Dinner of the States, which became the immensely popular and widely known All-States Picnic, held for the first time on Euclid Avenue in 1932, when the city celebrated its 50th anniversary. In 1948 it would record 150,000 people having dinner together at the event's mile-long picnic table, attracting national and international attention.

Other important activities of the time included the contribution of funds for the development of a city airport, which eventually would become Ontario International Airport; working on obtaining improved telephone service for the residents; and negotiating to reroute Southern Pacific freight trains that came from Los Angeles through Ontario every half-hour.

Following a major reorganization in 1936, the chamber began to function in a more structured and professional way than it had been able to previously. This change led, among other advances, to expanded programs in its three main areas of concern: issue-oriented, people-oriented, and community-oriented activities, which still are its primary objectives.

Today the Ontario Chamber of Commerce has more than 1,000 members and continues its dedication to ensuring a positive business environment in a city that is becoming the fastest-growing community in the Inland Empire.

This lavish display of Ontario's bountiful citrus crop was part of the Los Angeles Citrus Fair in the early 1900s.

Local downtown merchants' stores in the early 1900s were focal points of Ontario's small-town life. Some of the original merchants and buildings still remain in the downtown area. The City of Ontario has been active in restoring the historic structures.

DAISY WHEEL RIBBON CO., INC.

When Stephen and Sharon Baer decided in 1980 to sell typewriter ribbons, carbon paper, and duplicating supplies out of their garage, they were trying more to cope with circumstances than to become entrepreneurs. Stephen's employer, Columbia Ribbon and Carbon Company, a national manufacturer, had ceased doing business suddenly, leaving Stephen with customers who wanted product. As a popular and successful salesman, he had a loyal customer base on which he believed he could build an independent distributorship of his own.

Stephen had joined Columbia Ribbon and Carbon in 1966 and, following several transfers around the country, arrived at Columbia's branch factory in Rancho Cucamonga in 1975. In 1980 Stephen, who was in sales management, went back to doing what he really liked best, being a salesman on the road.

But the writing was on the wall for Columbia, and it was then that the Baers launched their own operation, Daisy Wheel Ribbon Co., Inc. They operated out of the garage for only four months before business reached a level where they needed more space and people. They rented a 1,500-square-foot facility and soon added two former Columbia employees, Lilly Ricks as office manager and Stan Moffitt in sales. Around the same time a new development took place. People began coming in the office to buy ribbons and other supplies, prompting the Baers to open a retail store in the building.

The young firm's sales continued to grow rapidly, although the emphasis had by then changed from duplicating supplies and typewriter ribbons to top brand-name computer ribbons and supplies.

The Baers rented a second and then a third unit until, in 1985, they faced a choice: either add a

From left are Stan Moffitt, sales; Lilly J. Ricks, office manager; Stephen W. and Sharon M. Baer, owners; and two of the five Baer children, Harold W. and Laura T. Baer.

fourth unit and occupy the entire 6,000-square-foot building, which still would be inadequate, or look for another building. They found the answer on East Shelby Street in Ontario, near Interstate 10 and Haven Avenue, where a 9,600-square-foot structure was for sale. Daisy Wheel Ribbon Co. purchased it. Only three years later the firm is again bursting at the seams, and new, larger quarters are being sought.

Daisy Wheel is also known as DWR Co., Inc., to better reflect the diversity of product lines it distributes. The firm continuously updates its inventory to include state-of-the-art merchandise, and currently stocks computer printer and typewriter ribbons, diskettes, laser and copier toners, facsimile (fax) and computer paper, labels, computer accessories, and more.

Today DWR's customers range from *Fortune* 1,000 firms to computer hobbyists and home-office workers. With annual gross sales of more than $4 million, the company employs 23 full-time workers. All five of the Baer children—Harold, Laura, Linda, Bess, and Bill—are involved to varying degrees in the thriving and still growing business.

Daisy Wheel Ribbon Co., Inc., is an uplifting example of how two resourceful and self-confident people can overcome adversity and turn it into an opportunity for great success.

DWR Co.'s inventory includes a complete line of computer, typing, and duplicating supplies.

THE ONTARIO CENTER

Rising on what was once expected to be the West Coast version of the Indianapolis Motor Speedway, The Ontario Center enters the 1990s as the premier multiuse community of the Inland Empire. Posed dramatically against the backdrop of the San Bernardino Mountains, the master-planned development is writing a vibrant chapter in the area's economic history.

From the beginning it had been decided that the new venture would have an attractive environment that would appeal to employers and employees alike and also be responsive to the needs of the community. To achieve that goal, The Ontario Center is a blending of office, entertainment, retail, and residential uses, with 100 acres set aside for parks, landscaped pathways and roads, and a 13-acre waterscaped view corridor.

A wholly owned subsidiary of Chevron Land and Development Company, whose parent organization is the Chevron Corporation, The Ontario Center is ideally located at the junction of Interstate 10 (San Bernardino Freeway) and Interstate 15 (Devore Freeway) and close

to Ontario International Airport. It is also at the hub of a large pool of employees, many of whom live nearby and until now have had no choice but to commute long distances to work.

Purchased in 1980, The Ontario Center underwent years of intensive research, planning, and site preparation before land parcels were ready to be offered for sale.

The development, which is divided into specific-phase sectors scheduled to continue through the year 2001, includes the creation of a financial district along the Haven Avenue corridor. It will feature regional headquarters for several major national financial institutions, corporate headquarters for regional financial institutions, and facilities for accountants, stockbrokers, mortgage lenders, and law firms.

Other phases at The Ontario Center include 159 acres of office de-

The 404-unit Park Centre Apartments—a joint venture with Western National Properties—is just one of the completed residential developments in The Ontario Center.

velopments with plazas and a pedestrian pathway; 186 acres of retail operations, such as restaurants, specialty shops, as well as a 150-acre, 1.9-million-square-foot super regional value-oriented specialty center named Ontario Mills to be built by Western Development Corporation of Washington, D.C.; 40 acres for hotels to serve businesses, tourists, and shoppers using Ontario International Airport and Ontario Mills; and 77 acres of medium-density, multifamily residential villages, with community enhancements that include a grammar school, a child-care facility, and a park.

Many of the projects for these designated land parcels either have

An aerial view of The Ontario Center as it will look when completed.

been completed or are under way, and represent a mix of Chevron/Ontario Center joint ventures and sales to other developers for specific uses. These projects include 45 residential four-plexes, a joint venture with Covington Homes; the 404-unit Park Centre Apartments, a joint venture with Western National Properties; and the Ontario Airport Hilton, a full-service hotel with 309 rooms and full conference facilities. The five office buildings include the four-story, 80,000-square-foot First Financial Center, owned and managed by O'Donnell, Armstrong & Partners; the three-story, 56,000-square-foot Haven Pointe, developed by The Sickels Group of San Diego; Palm Brook Corporate Center, two- and three-story buildings totaling 80,000 square feet, owned by Mission Viejo Company; the two-story, 40,000-square-foot Ontario Financial Plaza, developed by LeeLand Enterprises of Orange; and a 17,400-square-foot executive suite office building by Office Technology Group of Ontario.

The retail area includes Plaza Continental, a 191,000-square-foot specialty retail and restaurant complex with such anchor restaurants as El Torito, Stuart Anderson's Black Angus, and Spoons Bar & Grill. The complex was developed by Albert Auer & Associates of Newport Beach.

Also under development are a 15-screen movie complex, the second largest in the state, by Edwards Theatres Circuit, Inc.; six additional

The Ontario Motor Speedway, once the home of the California 500, has become The Ontario Center—a diverse mix of office, entertainment, retail, and residential facilities.

office buildings, including a 585,000-square-foot office park commencing with a nine-story, 195,000-square-foot building by American Trading Real Estate Properties, Inc., of Baltimore, Maryland; a 180,000-square-foot regional headquarters for Wells Fargo Bank; a new four-story, 43,500-square-foot corporate headquarters building for HMC Architects; a 50,000-square-foot, four-story atrium office building by Arical Properties of Costa Mesa; a 47,000-square-foot atrium office building by Sahama Investments of Rancho Cucamonga; and a 52,000-square-foot office building by Albert Auer & Associates. In addition to the 45 four-plex residen-

tial units completed by Covington Homes, 15 four-plex units will be completed in 1990. A 609-unit residential village by Hill Companies of Newport Beach is also scheduled for completion in 1991.

The Ontario Center, when completed, will boast, in addition to its office buildings, 2,250 hotel rooms, and more than 2 million square feet of retail space. Also planned are such amenities as an auto-service mall, a health club, and medical facilities. As one of Southern California GTE's SmartParks, The Ontario Center has been designed and planned to offer state-of-the-art telecommunications capabilities through its sophisticated fiber-optic systems.

Recognizing the heritage of the land's auto-racing days, The Ontario Center's interior streets have been given such names as Lotus, Duesenberg, and Bugatti, and the main east-west "G" Street is now known as Inland Empire Boulevard. While looking back to the area's past, the rapidly growing urban center is at the same time providing a look forward into tomorrow's business environment.

The Empire Towers at The Ontario Center.

BOB & ED'S GLASS

One of the oldest glass shops in the Ontario area, Bob & Ed's Glass was started in the 1950s by two former city fire fighters who saw an opportunity to provide an essential service to the rapidly developing residential and commercial community. They purchased land at 422 South Euclid Avenue and began operating out of a large facility that remains relatively unchanged to the present day.

Meanwhile, as the business built toward becoming a permanent and successful part of the city growing up around it, two other young men, who at the time had no inkling that they would own the company one day, crossed paths briefly as they sought to establish their separate careers.

Jim Smith, a native of Harrison, Arkansas, had been working in 1964 for Bob Hardy at Bob & Ed's Glass. But then Smith decided to become a partner himself in a retail glass shop, Smith Brothers Glass, located at 1136 West Holt in Ontario. He stayed there until 1968, when he returned to Arkansas and went to

work for Sutton Handle Factory.

When Smith left Smith Brothers, a Vietnam War veteran named Karl Vander Vies, who had been employed in the glass business in Buena Park from when he was a teenager until he entered the service, was hired. It would be two years before Smith and Vander Vies would meet again.

The Smiths returned from Arkansas in 1970, and the following year bought out Bob & Ed's Glass in partnership with Vander Vies. Soon they would change the direction of the firm from largely serving the construction industry to what it is today, a complete retail glass center.

As the years passed the company flourished and firmly established itself as a dependable source of quality workmanship and product. Bob & Ed's Glass provides and installs glass for a multitude of uses:

The office staff consists of Mary (seated) assisted by Shellie (left) and Carrie.

custom walls of mirrors, tub and shower enclosures, windows and patio doors, wardrobe mirror doors, and a full line of automotive windshields and side glasses. It specializes in contract glazing and apartment window replacements and will send a professional glazier to replace broken glass in homes and businesses.

Splitting the responsibilities, Smith operates the sales end of the business, assisted by his wife, Mary, and Vander Vies handles the outside home and commercial glass installation. Among the employees, Dwaine Moss, who has been with the company since 1975, is the shop manager, and the Smiths' two daughters, Carrie Johansen and Shellie Hoy, have part-time positions. The Smiths' have four grandchildren.

Bob & Ed's Glass has been a successful and satisfying partnership that reaches back more than 30 years into a history of reliability and service of a kind increasingly hard to find in these times of constant change.

Established in the 1950s, Bob & Ed's Glass has grown and prospered along with Ontario. Shown here are (from left) Dwaine, Karl, and Jim.

CALIFORNIA OCCUPATIONAL MEDICAL GROUP

Unlike most patients, when Paul Marc Umof was a child in Buffalo, New York, be found hospitals to be exciting places. That perception stayed with him, and when he was a young man in the 1960s, it became his springboard into a life that he felt would make a positive and lasting contribution to society.

He decided to become a physician, earning his Bachelor of Science in Medicine and Medical Doctor degrees from Northwestern University. He then headed west to California to do his internship and residency at UCLA's Harbor General Hospital. A man who "loves medicine and enjoys taking care of patients," he spent the next two years at Cedars Sinai Hospital before entering private practice in emergency medicine in Orange County.

He discovered his true destiny in 1982. While working as director of emergency service at Chino Community Hospital, he also joined the

Paul M. Umof, M.D., medical director of the California Occupational Medical Group and the Milliken Medical Group. He also serves as director of emergency services at the Chino Community Hospital.

staff of the first industrial medicine clinic in the area. Located on Archibald Avenue in Cucamonga, it had been founded in 1979 and was serving all of Ontario.

Seeing an opportunity to modernize and expand the health care programs provided to the fast-growing commercial community, Dr. Umof purchased the clinic in 1982. For the next three years he would put in backbreaking 80- to 90-hour weeks, "enjoying every minute of it," carefully nurturing the California Occupational Medical Group into what today consists of two major primary health care facilities specializing in industrial medicine. During that period he also serviced the emergency room at Anaheim Stadium.

The second clinic, Milliken Medical Group, opened in 1988 on a one-acre site at South Milliken Avenue near Jurupa in Ontario. Plans already are under way to add a third facility at Grove and Francis in Ontario and to transfer corporate headquarters to the Milliken location.

Today the clinics employ a full complement of primary care physicians, board-certified physician specialists, physicians' assistants, medical assistants, registered X-ray technicians, administrators, and office staff.

California Occupational Medical Group, located in Rancho Cucamonga, was established in 1979 as the first industrial medical clinic in the area. California Occupational Medical Group continues to be the forerunner in providing prompt, cost-effective, quality care in industrial medicine.

The practice serves a constantly increasing number of industries and businesses in the area, handling on-the-job injuries, pre-employment physicals, drug and alcohol testing, executive physicals, and back-to-work evaluations. It also offers neutral second medical opinions and treatment courses for insurance cases and functional capacity evaluations.

Board-certified in emergency medicine, Dr. Umof is chief of staff and head of the Medical Executive Committee at Chino Community Hospital and an active member of San Antonio Hospital's medical staff.

Dr. Umof is married, and he and his wife, Eugenia, have three daughters, Erika, Natalie, and Jaquelyne.

A caring, dedicated physician who has kept intact his early sense of excitement about the world of medicine, he is a modern-day pioneer contributing to the future of Ontario.

GLENN B. DORNING INC.

Visitors to Glenn B. Dorning Inc.'s industrial and agricultural equipment sales and service business on East Holt Boulevard in Ontario will not a see a group of overalled farmers huddled around a new tractor, eagerly discussing its merits while their horses stomp impatiently nearby. But it probably would not surprise them if they did, for that nostalgic atmosphere seems tangible despite the shiny new Massey-Ferguson equipment there.

For more than 40 years the company has operated out of the same unpretentious building, consistently offering the kind of old-fashioned personal attention and dependability that the hardheaded farmers of yesteryear demanded—and got—from Glenn B. Dorning himself when he started servicing their machinery.

Brought to Southern California from Kansas in 1921 by his father, Glenn graduated from college in 1930 into a Depression-plagued economy. He had two things going for him: farmers needed to keep their equipment running,

At the same location on East Holt Boulevard 40 years later, the staff of Glenn B. Dorning Inc. poses with (seated left to right) Glenn Rowlands, Glenn B. Dorning, and Sonny Rowlands.

and he was a good mechanic.

In 1936 he and his wife, Maxine, a bookkeeper, pooled their skills and went into business on Euclid Avenue to service and sell farm machinery. He became a subdealer for various lines of equipment and began to build a reputation for capability and in-depth product knowledge. But Pearl Harbor intervened, and Glenn, an amateur flyer, leased his business and entered the U.S. Air Force as a pilot instructor.

When he was discharged in 1945 he found the business in shambles and believed the only way he could rebuild it was to offer dependable service. His prewar customers remembered, and soon he was on his way again.

By 1947 he moved the company to its present two-acre site on East Holt, where he built a shop and sales floor and eventually added a warehouse. Then, in 1948, he took on the Massey-Ferguson line, the beginning of his firm's future success.

A 1950 photo shows the entire staff of Glenn B. Dorning Inc. With two mechanics are Glenn and Maxine Dorning (center) and Sonny Rowlands (far right).

As the years passed it became clear to Glenn that the economy of the Inland Empire was shifting rapidly from agriculture to industrial growth, and he became a distributor for paving, building, earth-moving, and light-industrial equipment. It was a good move, and today industrial machinery accounts for a majority of the company's business. Nevertheless, he has never forgotten where he started. Glenn B. Dorning Inc. continues as a dealer for farm machinery, some to original customers since relocated to often distant areas.

Glenn retired in 1971, succeeded by his nephew, Sonny Rowlands, who joined him in 1946 right out of the U.S. Navy, and Sonny's son, Glenn, as vice-president, keeping intact the future family's stewardship. The company has 23 employees and continues to grow as an award-winning Massey-Ferguson equipment and parts distributor and dealer.

Today, more than a half-century later, dependability is still the watchword of Glenn B. Dorning Inc.

FIRST AMERICAN TITLE INSURANCE COMPANY

When First American Title Insurance Company celebrated its 100th anniversary recently, it was doing more than just marking the passage of time. Founded in 1889 in Santa Ana, where it is still headquartered, the firm was looking back with well-deserved pride at its contributions to the opening and development of the West.

Settlers were flocking to California to take advantage of land grants, government auctions, private land sales, and other so-called opportunities, many of which turned out to be fraudulent. Then, as now, an orderly and dependable method of transferring land titles and protecting property ownership was needed.

Charles E. Parker, founder of Orange County Title Company, First American's predecessor, set out to build a conservatively run, financially sound service organization to meet these needs. He formed the new company by consolidating two existing abstract firms that were operating in Santa Ana.

Established only 13 years after the practice of title insurance began in the nation, the enterprise was to grow from two to today's 6,000 employees and a network of more than 2,500 branch offices, subsidiaries, affiliates, or agents in all 50 states and in Guam, Mexico, Puerto Rico, the Virgin Islands, and England.

In its more than a century of business, First American has had only five presidents—four of them members of the founding family. Charles E. Parker was followed by H.A. Gardener, who led the firm until C.E.'s son, George Parker, took over. In time, George's nephew and C.E.'s grandson, Donald Kennedy, succeeded to the presidency, and currently Parker Kennedy, Donald's son and great-grandson of the founder, is president and chief executive officer. This has provided the kind of continuity and dependability that C.E. Parker first envisioned.

As part of an aggressive expansion program in 1958, First American acquired controlling interest in the 10-year-old Land Title Company of San Bernardino, which had previously moved from its original location to the former Montgomery Ward Building. That structure was leveled in 1965 to provide a parking lot adjoining First American's present four-story, multimillion-dollar center at 323 Court Street, across from the county courthouse.

Regional vice-president C. Wayne Wood, who heads the 200-member staff in San Bernardino, joined the original local firm at its inception in 1948, along with vice-president Lorene Meek and vice-president and chief title officer Edward D. Young, who retired in 1989.

First American Title Insurance Company is an intrinsic part of the Inland Empire's history, serving today's needs with the same uncompromising philosophy of quality and values it offered to those early settlers so many years ago.

Founded in Santa Ana more than 100 years ago, First American Title Insurance Company still serves the Inland Empire with the same integrity that has reassured land buyers and owners over the years. Shown here is the landmark First American Title Building in San Bernardino.

TRANSAMERICAN PLASTICS CORPORATION

Successful ideas sometimes are deceptively simple. Often someone identifies and meets a need that, in retrospect, seems so obvious one wonders why nobody had ever done anything about it before. But that is what entrepreneurs are all about and how whole new worlds of opportunity are opened up. Transamerican Plastics Corporation in Ontario, today one of California's largest and most innovative manufacturers of a wide range of polyethylene products, started exactly that way.

A young man named Sam Chebeir, who had come to California in 1967 and, following college, went into sales for Mercedes-Benz of North America, decided to take an idea that had been percolating in his mind for some time and put it into action. Working with automobiles, he had become aware that there was no easy way to protect a new car's upholstery from being soiled during the vehicle's manufacture and later, when being serviced or having body or other repair work done.

The solution, Chebeir believed, was disposable automotive protective plastic coverings that he had invented and designed. Although the automobile industry had long been in existence and was introducing remarkable new technological advances each year, apparently no one had thought of how to deal with a problem that must have been perceived as something far down on the list of things to worry about. No one, that is, except Sam Chebeir.

In 1978 Chebeir founded Transamerican Plastics Corporation in a 1,000-square-foot plant in Los Angeles to manufacture and market his new disposable plastic coverings. Initially, his entire work force consisted of just himself and a secretary, but the response to his idea was immediate, and it was not long

before he was selling the product nationwide—a development that eventually would make the corporation the world leader it is today in automotive protective coverings.

By 1984 the company had prospered and grown to the point where it moved from Los Angeles to larger quarters in Whittier, where a line of plastic products was added to the automotive protective coverings to provide a diversity that would help to open up new markets.

It was a good decision, and in 1987, its sales still skyrocketing, Transamerican built its present 100,000-square-foot manufacturing, distribution, and headquarters facility on five acres on East Santa Ana Street in Ontario. The choice of Ontario was made following an intensive search for an ideal site.

Chebeir had been looking for a centrally located area from which to serve Southern California and the western United States and considered moving to Orange, Ventura, Riverside, or San Bernardino counties. Eventually, however, he selected Ontario because it seemed to offer the most of what he was seeking: the positive and supportive attitude of local government, reasonably priced land, an available labor force of good quality, a nearby network of major freeways, and the Ontario International Airport.

Transamerican also established

Sam Chebeir, president of Transamerican Plastics Corporation, founded the company upon innovative ideas and hard work.

two distribution centers in Michigan and Ohio, from which the company supplies its products to all 50 states. More than 100 people are employed by the firm.

Transamerican is also aggressively pursuing the international market and operates a plant in Colombo, Sri Lanka, and has a sales office in Tokyo, Japan.

Now a full-service and still-growing manufacturer of a line of standard polyethylene film and bags for a multitude of applications, Transamerican's research and development department each year also introduces dozens of custom-de-

ABOVE: Skyrocketing growth necessitated the construction of Transamerican Plastics' 100,000-plus-square-foot manufacturing, distribution, and headquarters facility on East Santa Ana Street.

LEFT: An interior view of Transamerican Plastics' plant in Ontario.

Chebeir credits his firm's phenomenal success to the team efforts of management and the insistence on quality as the top priority, beginning with the selection of only the finest raw materials available, such as those provided by Chevron, and continuing through the entire design and manufacturing processes. He also is proud of the firm's ability to produce an ever-growing array of improved products and applications—from developing new technology to the latest in co-extrusion processing—that has made it a standard-setter in the highly competitive plastics-packaging business.

The history of Transamerican Plastics Corporation, much like Ontario's own, records the kind of exciting progress that has been made possible by pioneering entrepreneurs such as Sam Chebeir—people who have the courage to go out on the cutting edge of the future with ideas they believe in.

Plastic film comes off the production line at Transamerican Plastics. State-of-the-art equipment and technology produce quality products that compete in a worldwide market.

signed specialty products for such industries as automotive, aerospace, construction, textiles, transportation, medical, food packaging, furniture, agriculture, and consumer and industrial packaging. It is one of the leading manufacturers of low- and high-density polyethylene film and bags including, but not limited to, anti-stat, flame-retardant, and stretch film. Chevron Chemical Company supplies Transamerican with its raw materials.

Chebeir is particularly pleased by Transamerican's relationship with Chevron, a company he says accurately reflects his own business philosophy. "We're demanding when it comes to our supplier's products," he says, "because we service such a wide variety of markets—highly specialized markets. We have to know the resins we buy are the same every time." What he likes about Chevron is that "it is as committed to our business as we are and understands the importance of providing the total package: the right product and the right people."

Transamerican is increasing its production capacity through an aggressive modernization program that includes using the latest, state-of-the-art equipment. The goal is to achieve faster production and turn-around time, greater diversity, and a superior-quality industrial film that is guaranteed to perform.

EMPLOYMENT TRAINING AGENCY OF THE WEST END

Uniquely tailored to meet the labor needs of the fast-growing business and industrial communities of western San Bernardino County, the federally funded Employment Training Agency (ETA) was created in 1973 with the City of Ontario as its administrative entity.

It was destined to make a major contribution to the explosive economic progress of the area, something that the cities of the west end and the County of San Bernardino had clearly foreseen when they spearheaded the efforts to establish the agency.

The idea to locate a program in Ontario had first been sparked by a problem perceived by the five west end cities—Ontario, Montclair, Chino, Rancho Cucamonga, Upland, and the San Bernardino County portion of Pomona. The Comprehensive Employment Training Act (CETA) agency was headquartered in San Bernardino at the time, placing a heavy commuting burden on west end stu-

ETA provides employees with an abundant labor pool of motivated, professionally skilled people of all ages.

dents, and the decision was made to petition for a closer office to serve them. Many were also critical of the CETA because they believed it tended to train people for minimal, temporary jobs, and they were convinced that a better way could be found to produce well-qualified local workers for businesses.

Soon afterward the West End Multi Service Center (the forerunner of today's Employment Training Agency) was opened in Ontario, the largest of the western Inland Empire's cities.

Headquartered at 1129 West Fourth Street in Ontario in a modern, 7,000-square-foot building, ETA serves the five cities under the leadership of director John Mooney. It has approximately 28 employees.

To employers, both those contemplating moving to the western Inland Empire and those already there, the agency offers local work-

ers trained at no cost to the company or on-the-job training of new employees with half of their salaries paid by the ETA for up to six months. In addition, for each eligible person hired, an employer can claim a tax credit of up to $3,000. The agency also is available to help a company with high turnover or affirmative action.

The only agency providing such services in the area, ETA is special in that it is very business and people oriented. It concentrates on pro-

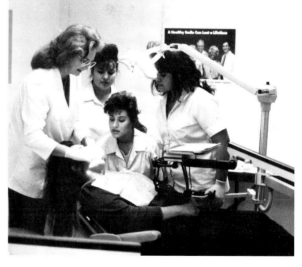

viding an abundant labor pool of motivated, professionally skilled and unskilled people of all ages, including machinists, computer operators, maintenance workers, clerks, medical technicians, airline/airport employees, and food-service workers.

ETA first finds out what particular skills an employer is seeking and then works with the company to design a training program for potential employees. What the client gets—at no cost—is prescreened, thoroughly tested, well-trained workers who meet the required needs of the company. The other option, the on-the-job training program, encourages businesses to use ETA's services to teach skills to new employees.

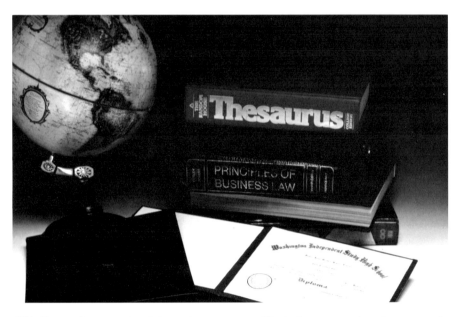

ETA allows students to work at their own pace toward a high school diploma or GED certificate.

Recent figures show that more than 80 percent of west end ETA's adult graduates were successfully employed, compared to the state's 56-percent employment quota. In one year alone, as many as 400 local area residents were regularly placed in jobs following ETA assessment and training.

The agency operates basic vocational training that is conducted through community colleges, adult schools, and private vocational schools, and includes retraining, resume preparation, job-search skills, and assistance in locating jobs for dislocated workers—all at no cost to the participant or employer. ETA also offers the Summer Youth Employment Program (SYETP) to prepare young people for jobs through federal, state, city, and nonprofit agencies; the Senior Citizen Program to provide vocational training for persons 55 years of age and older; and state-mandated training for individuals collecting Aid for Families with Dependent Children (AFDC), in accordance with Governor George Deukmejian's Workfare Program.

To help remove barriers to seeking training for employment, ETA offers child care and transportation assistance.

An important goal of the agency is to open doors for people seeking a brighter future, particularly those dreaming of a particular career but don't know how to pursue it, or those who need to complete their basic educational requirements. ETA personnel help candidates to discover their interests and test them for reading, math, and language abilities and, if necessary, provide assistance in upgrading skills they already have. For those who need better communication skills, English-as-a-Second-Language courses are available. Best of all, it is tuition-free education.

Using instructional computers at ETA's Learning Center, which has private carrels, students work at their own pace toward a General Education Development (GED) certificate or a high school diploma. Di-

plomas and GED certificates are awarded by Washington Independent High School through the Colton Unified School District and the Chino Adult School through the Chino Unified School District.

Lauded by local business people for the high caliber of its training and quality of its graduates, the Employment Training Agency of the West End covers an unusually wide range of services. But its own measure of success is the constantly increasing numbers of motivated, upward-bound, newly skilled employees who have been given a chance to create better, more productive lives for themselves. That is the real bottom line.

The ETA Learning Center has private carrels featuring instructional computers that help students achieve their educational goals.

SOUTHWEST CONCRETE PRODUCTS

An aerial view of the Southwest Concrete Products plant, which was taken in 1988.

Although America offers many readily identifiable entrepreneurial opportunities to those willing to take chances and work hard, some of the most successful ventures are notable for being ideas that would not occur to many people—areas such as the manufacture of precast concrete manholes, a product that is buried underground and seen only by those who work near them.

But to three young men whose job was installing manholes, the idea of actually making the product themselves seemed not only like an obvious and realistic challenge, but an opportunity to improve the industry.

Bob Dzajkich, his brother, Joe, and brother-in-law George Fricke had become increasingly frustrated by having to sit around waiting for constantly late deliveries of manholes to the construction sites where they worked. These delays were costly, and there had to be a better way of doing it, they rea-

soned. While they had no previous experience in manufacturing a product or running a plant, they felt confident they could build quality precast concrete manholes and deliver and install them on time. That, as it turned out, was probably the understatement of the year.

In 1966 the budding entrepreneurs opened Southwest Concrete Products for business on a 1.5-acre lot on South Benson Avenue in Ontario to manufacture and install precast manholes. By 1976 they were doing so well that they decided to drop the installation side of the operation and concentrate solely on the sale of their product.

The following year Bob Dzajkich and George Fricke bought Joe Dzajkich's shares in the company and, soon after, made another change in the direction of the growing venture

that would greatly expand the firm's marketing base. They began to buy and distribute other manufacturers' products, such as Contech truss pipe, fittings, manhole cast-iron rings, and covers, lines that now include hundreds of related items and account for a healthy share of Southwest's profits.

In addition to manufacturing standard and specialized precast manhole units of various sizes, Southwest Concrete Products also makes and sells plastic safety steps for use in manholes in Japan and the United States; it is the second firm in the nation to use a completely automated machine to fabricate these precast manholes with cast-in-place steps.

The company today is located on a 20-acre site right next door to where it was founded in 1966. It has approximately 27,000 square feet of manufacturing and office facilities and employs more than 40 people. Gross annual sales exceed $9 million.

Serving Southern California, Southwest Concrete Products has never forgotten its founders' philosophy: to provide prompt and dependable delivery of quality products to customers. To help accomplish that, it has specially equipped cab-over diesel trucks to minimize delivery and unloading time at the destination points. Remote-control booms enable close installation observation by highly skilled operators to reduce after-delivery handling of manhole sections.

The company possesses unique fabrication capabilities to provide fast manufacturing response for large and small projects at competitive prices. A professional staff is also available to offer technical assistance to customers on the products Southwest manufactures.

Chief executive officer and president Bob Dzajkich, born in Los Angeles, has come a long way since

Today Southwest Concrete Products has approximately 27,000 square feet of manufacturing and office facilities, and its gross annual sales exceed $9 million. Bob Dzajkich (right) is seen here with Professor Yull Brown with whom he is working on a new form of clean energy using ordinary tap water.

In 1966 Southwest Concrete Products opened to manufacture and install precast manholes. The firm was originally founded by three partners— Bob Dzajkich (right), his brother Joe (left), and George Fricke (not pictured). In 1967 Bob Dzajkich and George Fricke bought Joe Dzajkich's shares in the company.

he learned bricklaying from his father, Simun, who had arrived penniless in the United States from Croatia, Yugoslavia, and carved out his share of the American dream by supporting his family as a craftsman. Bob Dzajkich is assisted in the business by George Fricke, vice-president involved in almost every phase of operation and marketing at Southwest Concrete Products.

Looking to the future with the same enlightened enthusiasm he had when he started the company, Bob Dzajkich is exploring a new form of clean energy. Simply put, by using ordinary tap water, a method has been developed in a laboratory by Professor Yull Brown, a researcher from Australia. This process separates water using D.C. electrolysis into a stoichiometric mixture of hydrogen and oxygen. This completely safe, pollution-free gas is implosive not explosive, therefore creating an economical vacuum.

The new gas causes aluminum alloy to fuse at 600 degrees Celsius and, without adjustment of the flame in either size of intensity, sublimates tungsten steel at 6,000 degrees Celsius. So unique and cost efficient, this gas can destroy toxic waste with no smokestack, no more pollution.

Working with Professor Brown, who has patents in 31 industrial countries, Southwest hopes to bring the professor to the United States and help him gain U.S. citizenship. Bob Dzajkich also has an active interest and involvement in the future potential uses of the new energy process in other areas.

Southwest Concrete Products, born out of a frustration that three men translated into an opportunity, has flourished and grown to be an important part of the industrial development of Ontario and the Inland Empire.

SAN ANTONIO ORCHARD COMPANY

When young Charles "Charlie" Latimer founded San Antonio Orchard Company in Ontario in 1912, he started an enterprise that would go far beyond a dream first begun by his father, Hugh, who had emigrated with his family from Ottawa, Canada, in 1890 to become a citrus rancher in Riverside.

Before arriving in Southern California, the elder Latimer had purchased, sight unseen, a 40-acre orange grove in Riverside. He lived on and worked the land for several years before selling it to Sherman Indian Institute. Meanwhile, he had acquired other orchards in Riverside and Ontario.

Charlie, who as a youth helped his father in the citrus groves, went to work in 1906 in the Ely Gilmore packinghouse in Riverside. Only 19, he became the youngest manager in the industry at that time. Later he returned to his father's employ in the Ontario orchards. The orchards were approximately one mile west of Euclid Avenue, covering the area between today's Fourth Street and the San Bernardino Freeway. He stayed there until he founded San An-

tonio Orchard Company (named after nearby Mount San Antonio), and built a packinghouse on land leased from the railroad.

Across the street from the packinghouse was Latimer Field, the area's first airport and the forerunner of Ontario International Airport. The field was leased in the early 1920s from the Los Angeles and Salt Lake Railroad, now the Union Pacific Railroad.

In 1912 Charlie married Winifred Smith, daughter of W.W. Smith, mayor and city treasurer of Ontario in its early days. Charles

Charles Latimer (in the foreground) inspects the packing line. Latimer was president of the San Antonio Hospital Board of Trustees at the time of his death in 1950 and had previously served on the Ontario City Council.

was only 25 years old, but would in time make a profound contribution to the history and progress of the community.

Over the years Charlie continued to expand his business by adding other ventures to his citrus operation. In the years following World War I, the Ontario area continued as a major grape-growing cen-

San Antonio Orchard Company employees in 1925.

ter, and during Prohibition Latimer shipped and marketed grapes nationwide for juice and homemade wine. Building on that success—in some years he shipped as many as 750 railroad carloads of grapes—he became a broker and distributor for locally

RIGHT: The Ontario packinghouse in 1914, two years after its founding.

BELOW: Each year San Antonio Orchard Company ships from its Riverside packinghouse 300 containers of oranges that are exclusively from its own orchards to the Hong Kong market. Each container is the equivalent of a railroad car.

grown potatoes and dried fruits, particularly raisins. Meanwhile, he continued to ship oranges as his main crop.

Charlie also accumulated holdings in Riverside, Cucamonga, and San Diego County, where he grew oranges, lemons, grapes, avocados, and other agricultural products.

Joining him in these activities were his three sons—Wilbur H. "Bill" Latimer, today running the company; the late Charles R. "Chuck," who was the first elected mayor of Ontario; and John S. "Jack," who was killed in action with the U.S. Army in the Philippine Islands just a few days before the end of World War II.

Before Charlie Latimer died on March 8, 1950, at the age of 63, he

had become a prominent and successful figure in the citrus industry. He was chairman of the Distribution Committee of the first Federal Marketing Order (pro rate), a director of the Agricultural Producers, a director of the Gage Canal Company, and a director of the California Vineyard Association. His contributions to the Ontario area were legion. They included his tenure as a member of the Ontario City Council and the San Antonio Community Hospital Board of Trustees, of which he was president at the time of his death. A wing of the hospital bears his name today.

His interests also extended beyond the citrus business; he owned and bred thoroughbred horses, and he was a director of the California Thoroughbred Breeders Association.

His wife, Winifred, who was born in Ontario in 1887 and lived there until she died at age 77, was also active in the community. Described as "a wonderful, genteel, and cultured woman," she was a lifelong member of the First Methodist Church of Ontario and a member of the Friday Afternoon Club.

Mrs. Latimer took great pride in being the daughter and then mother of a mayor of Ontario.

Today San Antonio Orchard Company, still headquartered in Ontario, continues its 78-year history as an independent citrus grower, packer, and shipper, and now specializes in selling navel oranges in Asia, an idea the company pioneered in response to a changing market. Each year the firm ships from its Riverside packinghouse to Hong Kong approximately 300 containers of oranges that are exclusively from their own orchards. Each container is the equivalent of one railroad car. The firm shares in the top 10 percent of that market, with smaller amounts sent to Singapore and Malaysia. It still packs under the original labels of San Antonio Blue and San Antonio Red.

The firm at peak season—January to May—employs approximately 125 people and is headed by Bill Latimer, assisted by his son-in-law, Rick Starratt, manager, and Bill's daughters, Maggie Latimer-Starratt and Melissa Latimer-Lasiter.

A detractor once referred to Charlie Latimer as "a big toad in a small pond." The many who know his legacy increasingly appreciate Charles Latimer's knowledge, foresight, energy, and talents.

LOCKHEED AIRCRAFT SERVICE COMPANY

Headquartered at Ontario International Airport, Lockheed Aircraft Service Company (LAS) is the oldest and most diversified operation of its type in the United States. It is devoted to the maintenance, overhaul, repair, and modification of aircraft, involving structural changes and high-technology systems engineering. It is also the largest overseas-operating division of the Lockheed Corporation.

In 1933 Lockheed started a customer-service desk in Burbank when the twin-engined Electra was introduced to airline service. But by 1937 it was clear that more than a desk was needed, and a small customer-service department manned by 12 employees was established, using personnel, tools, and equipment that were mostly borrowed from other company divisions. Within a year the operation had tripled to 36 people with service and parts responsibility for more than 300 commercial Model 10 Electras, Model 12 Electra Juniors, and Model 14 Super Electras—100 of them in the United States and Canada and the rest scattered over five continents.

The firm's first modification job was creating the Lodestar by cutting the fuselage of an earlier Lockheed model and adding a 66-inch section. It was the beginning of airframe modification without degradation of flight integrity, a hallmark of LAS that continues into the jet age.

In 1938 Lockheed received one of its first major overseas assignments: to reassemble 200 Hudson bombers that were purchased by the British and shipped by freighter to Liverpool. Shortly after Pearl Harbor—using office space leased from Disney Studios in Burbank—Lockheed began recruiting personnel and procuring equipment for its expanding overseas operations. During World War II some 1,300 employees would work on 13,000

planes at Speke Air Force Base in Liverpool, and others would spend literally millions of hours repairing and maintaining thousands of aircraft at bases in Scotland and northern Ireland.

When the war ended, technological complexity continued to grow, necessitating the establishment of a wholly owned subsidiary, Lockheed Aircraft Service, Inc. LAS was immediately sought by many customers, notably in Iceland, to run the entire operation and maintenance of Keflavik Airport and to serve others at MacArthur Field in Long Island and Shannon Airport in Ireland. In 1949, when its MacArthur Field operation was moved to what is now John F. Kennedy International Airport, LAS began providing services that ranged from turnaround to major overhaul for most of the world's leading commercial airlines, sometimes

RIGHT: LAS developed the first Federal Aviation Administration (FAA)-approved flight data recorder in 1958. Today newer and more advanced units are manufactured at the LAS facility in Upland.

BELOW: U.S. Navy P-2V patrol aircraft received maintenance and modification on the flight line at LAS-Ontario in the 1950s.

working on 8,000 planes annually.

It was in New York that Lockheed workers converted a C-121 Constellation into the famous *Columbine I* for President Dwight D. Eisenhower. Earlier, they had produced a modified Douglas C-54, Franklin D. Roosevelt's *Sacred Cow,* and Harry Truman's DC-6 *Independence.* John F. Kennedy, Lyndon Johnson, and Richard Nixon also would have their presidential aircraft modified and maintained by LAS.

The firm became heavily involved in international programs in Zambia, Singapore, Ireland, Scotland, Germany, Saudi Arabia, and Greece. In Saudi Arabia, Lockheed fought severe mountain cold, scorch-

ABOVE: Maintenance completed, a C-130 Hercules aircraft awaits the arrival of a U.S. Air Force flight crew at the LAS facility in Chino.

RIGHT: A typical flight line scene at LAS-Ontario during the 1950s as dozens of F-94 aircraft received maintenance and modification by LAS technicians and craftsmen.

ing desert heat, and devastating sandstorms to maintain the kingdom's fleet of C-130 Hercules cargo aircraft. The company also developed a fleet of emergency hospital aircraft with short-distance takeoff and landing capabilities for remote areas, combined with sophisticated in-flight life support systems and surgical facilities. Presently LAS has overseas projects in Malaysia, Egypt, and China.

At home, Lockheed has converted the C-141 Starlifter into a flying laboratory for NASA, enabling the modified aircraft to carry a 15,000-pound, porthole-mounted infrared telescope to an altitude of 40,000 feet. Major projects at Ontario also include making fuel-saving alterations to the L-1011 and becoming the world leader in production of flight data recorders used to determine the cause of aircraft incidents and accidents.

Although basically a mainte-

nance organization for many years, Lockheed Aircraft Service Company today is a specialized, high-technology operation employing 1,000 people in its engineering department and more than 5,000 people overall in its Ontario; Greenville, South Carolina; and Arlington, Texas, subsidiaries. It also fields special teams to go where needed, in the United States or overseas. Most of the work done at the 70-acre Ontario facility is classified, dealing with the design, systems integration, and modification of aircraft into special airborne platforms for electronic warfare, command, control, and communications.

When Lockheed expanded to Ontario from its original Burbank location in 1952, it occupied two small, leased hangars surrounded by vineyards. Two years later the operation had become so well established that it was made the firm's headquarters.

Over the years LAS has worked on nearly 200,000 aircraft from 22 countries, with highly skilled mechan-

ics and technicians capable of handling single-engine, piston-driven planes at one end to multiengine jumbo jets at the other. The firm's basic tenet is to provide outstanding service to its customers, and it takes pride in its experience and ability to modify aircraft at only a fraction of the cost of manufacturing a new plane.

From its base in Ontario, Lockheed Aircraft Service Company, in addition to its work in the United States, has become a world leader in supplying aviation and ground-support services to foreign countries, helping them to achieve technical and economic security.

LOUD ENGINEERING AND MANUFACTURING, INC.

Like many successful businessmen, F.D. "Don" Whitehead, owner and president of Loud Engineering and Manufacturing, Inc., in Ontario, had the good fortune to work for someone who would profoundly influence the direction of his career.

An alumnus of Chaffey Junior College and Brigham Young University, Whitehead was unsure of what he wanted to do with his life. For the next few years he worked at Vortox, a manufacturer of air-cleaner filter systems in Claremont; General Dynamics, then located at the Los Angeles Fairgrounds; and Douglas Aircraft in Ontario, where he developed the background that helped prepare him for the significant next step he would take.

In 1953 Whitehead joined H.W. Loud Machine Works in Pomona, a manufacturer of landing gears for aircraft. It was there he met A.R. "Lance" Loud, the role model and mentor whom he still reveres as a father figure. Loud assigned him to handle contracts and sales, a position that led to his becoming vice-president and provided him with

the knowledge, skills, and contacts that would enable him to found his own business.

Loud Machine Works purchased Western Design in Montebello in 1960. Then, in 1963, National Distillers bought out Lance Loud and operated the company until 1967, when it was sold to Howmet Corporation.

Whitehead continued on as an executive during the changes of ownership, but in 1969, when Howmet sold the company to a competitor, he decided it was time to leave. Shortly thereafter, in May 1971, he founded Loud Engineering and Manufacturing, Inc., in an old winery building at 1427 South Garey Avenue in Pomona, which was formerly B.H. Hadley Co. He chose to adopt the Loud name, still known worldwide. There were only three employees: Whitehead, his wife, Helen (whom he had met at Loud Machine Works when she was secretary to vice-president T.A. Needham), and Don Forrest.

A recession had hit the aircraft industry, but it enabled Whitehead

to purchase equipment at various auctions to use in the overhaul of nose gear steering units for various military aircraft. Over the next seven years business prospered, and in late September 1978 the firm moved to its present location, a building it had purchased on a five-acre site at 1055 East Francis Street.

Loud Engineering and Manufacturing, Inc., continued to grow. Today it has three buildings consisting of 100,000 square feet, 150 employees, and gross annual sales of $9 million. The company designs, manufactures, and overhauls landing gear, actuators, and valves for such aircraft as the SR-71, TR-1, CH46, and CH47. It manufactures landing gear and nose gear steering units for the entire family of F-5 fighter planes. The firm's major customers include Lockheed, Boeing, Northrop, McDonald Douglas, the U.S. government, plus many foreign governments.

Loud Engineering and Manufacturing has been located at this five-acre site at 1055 East Francis Street since 1978.

POMONA DIE CASTING CORP.

When M.F. "Pete" and Doris Pierce celebrated their 50th wedding anniversary on September 2, 1989, they were able to look back with special satisfaction on a unique partnership in both marriage and business. Together, they had taken a dream and given it form and substance through hard work and an unwavering belief in their own abilities.

Like many of the successful entrepreneurs who have helped write the history of the area, Pete arrived in Southern California from the Midwest. His father, Harry Pierce, an auto mechanic, took his family from Lewellen, Nebraska, to Alhambra in 1922.

Doris' family had also moved to Southern California in the early 1920s. Her father, Roland T. Williams, had been a CPA for Texaco

Pete Pierce (left) consults with Robert Caudillo, an engineer and tool- and die-maker who has worked for Pomona Die Casting Corp. for 35 years.

in the Philippines, where she was born, and later in Japan. After returning to the United States, Williams attended law school and became an attorney in Los Angeles.

In 1944 Pete, who was a tool and die maker, entered the U.S. Air Force, serving as a flight engineer on B-29s until his discharge in 1946. He went back to his trade, working for several firms over the next six years. In 1952 he decided to start his own company, Pomona Molds, Inc., on State Street in Pomona, with his wife and two partners to engineer and build molds for the die-casting industry. The business prospered, and in 1953 Pete formed another company, Pomona Die Casting Corp., at the same location.

Soon after, H.L. "Red" Harvill, the "granddaddy" of the tool and die industry in Southern California, became a stockholder with the Pierces, the two other original partners now no longer associated with the firm. Both operations continued to

Pete Pierce, founder of the firm, was named "Man of the Year" in 1980 by the Society of Die Casting Engineers.

grow and, in 1957, were moved to a 3.5-acre site at 1218 East Airport Drive in Ontario, the present location. Harvill decided to retire in 1965 and the Pierces bought him out, making them the sole stockholders. Then, in 1978, the two firms were merged under the Pomona Die Casting Corp. name.

The company designs molds and makes die castings in aluminum and zinc for a wide variety of products that range from low-voltage outdoor lighting, heater control valves, medical equipment, and carburetors for small engines such as weed-eaters and chain saws.

Pete and Doris have three daughters—Linda, Nancy, and Paula—and two grandchildren. Paula now helps run the business. They are especially proud to have an engineer and tool- and die-maker, Robert Caudillo, who has worked for the company for 35 years.

Pete was named "Man of the Year" in 1980 by the Society of Die Casting Engineers, but he considers the greatest reward of all to be his life and business partner, Doris.

MARK CHRISTOPHER CHEVROLET

There are not many high school seniors who know exactly what they want to do with their lives after graduation. And there are fewer still who manage to turn their dreams into the kind of success attained by Chuck Leggio, president of four thriving automobile dealerships, flag-shipped by Mark Christopher Chevrolet on East "D" Street in Ontario.

In 1961, immediately after he received his diploma from Garner High School in Bakersfield, Leggio went to work in sales for Three-Way Chevrolet. Within a year he had been promoted to used-car manager and three years later to general sales manager. Although still in his twenties, he became general manager in 1970, a remarkable accomplishment by any standard.

For the next five years Leggio ran the dealership, until, in 1975, he finally felt ready to strike out on his own and purchased the Bob Hicks Chevrolet franchise on West Holt Boulevard in Ontario. He shaped it into such a flourishing enterprise that by 1981 he was able to build a state-of-the-art facility at the corpora-

tion's present location on 13 acres of land just south of the San Bernardino Freeway.

Strongly family oriented, Leggio expressed his sentiments by naming the company Mark Christopher Chevrolet after his two young sons, Mark and Christopher, and he refers to the enterprise as "the dealership of the future." His goal is to do such a good job of implementing his unwavering policy of serving his customers just as he himself would want to be served, that his sons will one day inherit a dependable core of satisfied repeat buyers.

Both sons worked at the dealership after school, washing cars, cleaning floors, helping in the parts and service operations—in short, learning the business from the bottom up. When they graduated from Loyola University, they went to work full time at Mark Christopher Chevrolet. Today Mark is used-car sales manager, and Chris is new-car sales manager. Also, in keeping with the family-based philosophy, their

Mark Christopher Auto Center, Chevrolet, Geo, and Subaru is currently located here at the Vineyard Avenue exit, just off the I-10 Freeway in Ontario.

mother, Shirley, holds the post of corporate vice-president.

Chuck Leggio, meanwhile, continued to expand his growing empire, adding Mark Chris Subaru in 1984, adjacent to his Chevrolet operation on the Ontario property. He acquired an Oldsmobile dealership in Corona in 1986 (which he sold in 1989), an Acura franchise in Bakersfield in 1988 (Mark Chris Acura), and the Ted Williams Oldsmobile dealership in Santa Barbara in 1989 (now Mark Chris Olds/Cadillac/Subaru). Since then he has opened a new operation in Ontario for Geo, a General Motors' automobile, and built a special facility to service recreational vehicles.

Recently, Mark Chris Subaru has been rated number one in retail sales in Subaru's western region (California, Arizona, and Nevada) and number five in the nation. Mark Christopher Chevrolet has been ranked among the top 50 Chevrolet dealers in the western region and the leading 100 in the United States—not bad for a young high school student who had a dream nearly 30 years ago.

This picture of the first home of Mark Christopher Chevrolet was taken in 1975. The dealership was located on Holt Boulevard in Ontario.

CHINO VALLEY BANK

Chino Valley Bank's main office in Chino was built in 1977.

In 1974 George Borba, a Chino dairyman, felt that big banks had become too impersonal in their dealings with customers, so he and his brother, John, also a dairyman, brought five other men together to start what would become one of the great recent success stories of the Inland Empire and the San Gabriel Valley: Chino Valley Bank.

The five men who joined the Borba brothers were Ronald Kruse, John Lo Porto, John Vander Schaaf, Paul Cortez, and Charles Magistro. Today all except Cortez, who has retired, continue to serve on the bank's board of directors, with George Borba as chairman and Kruse as vice-chairman. Also serving on the board is John Cavallucci, president and chief executive officer.

The ambitious venture got under way in a 4,500-square-foot modular building on Central Avenue in Chino with a staff of 14 people, including three officers. Within the first two months the bank had attracted 1,500 checking accounts and deposits of more than $850,000. By the end of 1974 deposits had jumped to more than $2 million and total assets to nearly $4 million. "There was no turning back after that," says John Cavallucci, who has been president and chief executive officer since 1980. In time those figures

would reach today's deposits of more than $435 million and assets of in excess of $475 million, making it the largest independent bank headquartered in San Bernardino and Riverside counties.

Between 1981 and 1987 the bank pursued an aggressive expansion program, opening branches in East Chino, Colton, Pomona, Covina, San Bernardino, Arcadia, South Arcadia, and San Gabriel, a program begun in 1977 with the addition of a branch in Corona and others in Upland and Ontario in 1980. The following year it became a subsidiary of CVB Financial Corp., a newly organized holding company designed to reinforce the bank's ability to meet customers' needs for a broad range of financial services. Then, in 1987, it established the Ontario

Airport office, moved its corporate headquarters from Chino to Ontario, and opened a new data center the following year. The Riverside Business Center opened in 1990. These 14 branch offices, as well as the construction loan and accounts receivable departments, meet the needs of an ever-growing customer base.

In 1981 the bank changed from a retail operation to one largely concentrating on business and professional customers. As it was from the very beginning, however, the bank continues to be hallmarked by a friendly, people-oriented philosophy that provides its strength.

Today the incredible success of Chino Valley Bank as a David in an industry of Goliaths is a testimonial to the perceptive determination of seven men who refused to accept the status quo.

Pictured in front of the bank's new corporate office in Ontario are (from left) John Cavallucci, president and chief executive officer, and George Borba, chairman of the board.

MITSUBISHI CEMENT CORPORATION

When Mitsubishi Cement Corporation established its headquarters on East "D" Street in Ontario in 1988, it was creating its own niche in history as the first venture into the U.S. cement industry by the global network of widely diversified organizations known as the Mitsubishi Group of Companies.

In March of that year the new corporation completed its purchase of the 790-acre Cushenbury Cement Plant in the Mojave Desert, along with distribution facilities in Phoenix, Arizona, and Long Beach, California. The Ontario-based enterprise, which includes the MCC Development Corporation, had been formed by Mitsubishi Mining and Cement Co. Ltd., which traces its

own roots back to 1871 in Japan and the Mitsubishi Corporation, Mitsubishi Metal Corporation, The Mitsubishi Bank Ltd., and Mitsubishi Trust and Banking Corporation.

Today the firm has nearly 100 joint ventures, 124 wholly owned subsidiaries, and more than 600 overseas sales and manufacturing bases. Mitsubishi was founded more than a century ago as a shipping service integrating the islands of Japan through the transfer of goods from area to area and from industry to industry. The Mitsubishi companies, once managed by a central office, grew out of those activities. A period of restructuring led to the formation of Mitsubishi as it is now: a collection of independently managed corpo-

rations all dedicated to a common goal of excellence and reliability.

Mitsubishi Cement Corporation's limestone quarry is located adjacent to the Cushenbury plant, eight miles south of Lucerne Valley. Formerly owned by Kaiser Cement Corporation, the plant continues its role as an integral part of the community and its economy.

Over the years the Cushenbury plant has gone through a number of stages of expansion and modernization. In 1982 a new preheater/precalciner kiln rated at 5,000 tons per day was installed, becoming the largest production kiln in the United States. Also installed at that time were a new tertiary crusher, raw mill, finish mill, and a coal-processing system. Since then other improvements have been made by Mitsubishi Cement Corporation, which today produces and sells more than 1.6 million tons of high-quality cement annually to the construction industry.

The corporation has a simple philosophy that it presents to its employees: establish a solid business foundation by building mutual respect and developing and producing quality products. This is intended to create long-term loyalty of customers, mutual prosperity for the company and its employees, and respect from the community. It is a policy symbolized by the well-known Mitsubishi three-diamond trademark that originated in the flag of the founding shipping company and was adopted in 1910. Although the worldwide company is involved in widely differing businesses, the symbol is designed to represent the business spirit of all of its employees.

At the end of 1988 Mitsubishi Cement Corporation, through MCC

Mitsubishi Cement Corporation's first venture into the U.S. cement industry began in 1988.

Development Corporation, a wholly owned subsidiary of Mitsubishi Mining and Cement, Mitsubishi Corporation, and Mitsubishi Metal Corporation, acquired a 100-percent interest in Nevada Ready Mix Concrete Corporation of Las Vegas, Nevada. This action was followed in 1989 by the establishment of a 50-percent partnership with Owl Rock Products. Owl annually produces 8 million tons of aggregate and approximately one million cubic yards of concrete.

Also in 1989 Mitsubishi acquired a 30-percent interest in San Diego-based Escondido Ready Mix Concrete Inc., which produces 1.5 million cubic yards of concrete yearly and operates a single aggregate deposit.

Mitsubishi Mining and Cement Co. Ltd. is one of the oldest members of the Mitsubishi group. Engaged in the mining and development of such natural resources as coal and nonferrous metal ores, it entered the cement industry in 1954 and today is one of the leading cement companies in Japan. It has also extended operations into other fields, including advanced ceramics to develop components for the electronics industry, bioceramic products such as artificial bones and dental roots, the production of chemicals from seawater, and consulting and engineering services for cement industry-related projects overseas.

Mitsubishi Corporation, a worldwide enterprise engaged in general trading and diversified services, has more than 230 offices in more than 80 countries. It is aggressively expanding into new areas, such as information processing, telecommunications, biotechnology, electronics, space technology, and new materials.

Mitsubishi Metal Corporation is one of Japan's largest and most comprehensive nonferrous metals companies, active in smelting, refining, and fabricating. It also operates an extensive research and development program focused on advanced fabricating of nonferrous metals, new materials, and nuclear technology.

The addition of Mitsubishi Cement Corporation headquarters to Ontario's rapidly growing industrial and business base has helped bring a global focus and new prosperity to an area whose horizons once were limited to citrus orchards and vineyards.

The employees of Mitsubishi Cement Corporation.

KAWACO INC.

In some ways the story of Yo and Marcia Kawa brings to mind Giacomo Puccini's opera, _Madame Butterfly_—but without the sadness that dramatized that bittersweet romance between East and West. Marcia and Yo first met by happenstance one day in 1978. She was an attractive, fair-haired young woman working for a company that had hired Yo, a land-grading operator, U.S. Army veteran of the Korean War, and a first-generation American of Japanese descent.

The chemistry was instant and within a year led to their marriage and eventually to a working partnership in an increasingly successful business in Ontario.

It all began when Yo's father, Ike Kawaguchi, emigrated to the United States from Japan to start a farm in Utah. Like many immigrants, his goal was to become well enough established so that he could send for his family. He did well and was able to bring his wife, Jun, to join him in America.

Mrs. Kawaguchi, of ancient Japanese dynasty lineage, was unprepared for the hard field work demanded by the farm, but she soon adapted to the new life. In time they would have 12 children, all of whom worked beside their parents, and the farm prospered. It was there also, as a child, that Yo learned to operate and take care of tractors, skills that later would allow him to start his own successful business.

After leaving the farm and serving in the U.S. Army, Yo worked as a land grader for Mia Brothers in Ogden,

Utah, and, after moving to Southern California in 1961, did the same thing for Alexander & Howard. Then, in 1968, he started his own land grading company in Buena Park, an operation that by 1978 he was operating out of Anaheim with three tractors and Ken Lambourne, his soon-to-be son-in-law. Memories of this time were warmed by Yo's kindness to the unemployed and untrained.

In the years following his marriage to Marcia the business continued to grow. In 1988 Kawaco Inc., now with 13 tractors and 25 employees, moved into a new building at its present location at 1355 South Parkside Place in Ontario.

Providing grading for industrial, commercial, and residential projects in Los Angeles, San Bernardino, Riverside, and Orange counties, Kawaco Inc. today serves such major clients as Warmington Homes,

Hunco Development, and West Venture Homes.

In a compatible sharing of responsibilities, Yo is president, handling all of the field work, and Marcia is vice-president, running the firm's business affairs. The couple has four children—Tracy, Sherri, Randy, and Micah—and four grandchildren. Marcia, an entrepreneur in her own right, also has a business—Marlee—that sells parts for heavy-equipment and construction job site supplies.

For Yo and Marcia Kawa, it has been a marriage of personalities and talents that, unlike the fateful couple of Puccini's opera, has a happy ending.

Yo and Marcia Kawa with David Clevenger, working at a condominium project on Weir Canyon Road in Anaheim in 1985.

CALIFORNIA COMMERCE CENTER AT ONTARIO

If George and William Chaffey, brothers and engineers from Canada who in 1883 established the agricultural community that would become Ontario, were able to return today they would be amazed by what has happened to the citrus groves and their rural way of life. They would see thousands of acres covered by new industrial, commercial, and residential buildings, many completed and occupied and others under construction, bringing an explosive new prosperity and vitality to the area.

The Chaffeys would also see the California Commerce Center at Ontario, a 3,400-acre master-planned business park, the largest in the Inland Empire and the second largest in Southern California.

California Commerce Center at Ontario, the Inland Empire's largest business park, will be east and south of Ontario International Airport and will look like this artist's conception when it is complete in the mid-1990s. Phases I, II, III, and IV and the Ontario Auto Center lie east of the airport; the 505-acre California Commerce Center South is at the left in the photo. The Commerce Center is ringed by the San Bernardino, Ontario, and Pomona freeways.

Credited with setting the pace for industrial development in the Inland Empire since land sales began in 1983, the business park has helped create a new awareness of the Ontario International Airport region as a highly desirable location. It is Foreign Trade Zone 50-1, the largest privately owned foreign trade zone in the West and the only one in Southern California offering land parcels for sale and large buildings for lease.

The record is remarkable. Between 1983 and 1990 California Commerce Center's land sales totaled $163.4 million as the project's first 271-acre phase and second 292-acre phase were sold out, and the 95-acre Ontario Auto Center filled to capacity. Land sales in the 374-acre phase three began in the summer of 1990. The same success has continued at California Commerce Center South, a 505-acre 1986 addition to the original 1,350 acres that was placed on the market early in 1988.

Late in 1988 an additional 130 acres in the Ontario Center were acquired from Chevron Land and Development Company to be developed as California Commerce Center North, with land sales to begin in 1990.

The master developer of the California Commerce Center at Ontario is The Lusk Company of Irvine, one of the largest and oldest industrial, commercial, and residential developers in Southern California.

An interest in the center is also held by Donald W. Shaw of Newport Beach, who has been in real estate development for more than 40 years and has built more than 10 million square feet of industrial and commercial buildings, and Mission Land Company, a subsidiary of SCEcorp, parent company of Southern California Edison. Mission Land is a partner with Lusk in California Commerce Center North.

Presiding over the incredible growth of California Commerce Center at Ontario is David W. Ariss, managing director since 1984. He estimates that upon completion of the entire project, the center will have 30 million square feet of buildings with a valuation of more than $2.5 billion and will employ 35,000 people.

David W. Ariss, managing director of the California Commerce Center.

MACLIN MARKETS INC.

What had been treeless sand dunes in Chino in 1926 was transformed into this productive ranch by Lawrence "Mac" Maclin (second from right), his wife, Mable (center), and Don Nyberg (far left).

Spread across 40 acres in the agricultural preserve between Ontario and Chino is a unique enterprise that offers an unbeatable combination of the family fun of an old-fashioned country fair and the always satisfying thrill of finding a good bargain.

The site is now one of three similar outdoor markets owned by Maclin Markets Inc., but for more than 50 years the original enterprise has been better known to its countless thousands of visitors as the Chino Auction (the livestock auction on site continues to operate every Tuesday). Maclin Open Air Markets are a big step up from usual swap meets and flea markets.

It all began in 1926, when Lawrence "Mac" Maclin migrated to Southern California from Arkansas to start a dairy farm, grow crops, and raise and sell cattle. He bought the present site of Chino Auction and Open Air Market, land that was then treeless sand dunes, and transformed it into a productive ranch.

But the area in which he was most successful was his extraordinary ability to sell his cattle. Soon other farmers were coming from miles around to ask him to do the same for them. It suggested to him an opportunity too good to pass up, and in 1936 Maclin decided to leave farming and go full time into the cattle-auction business. He formed the Maclin-Caldwell Auction Company with Harold Caldwell, a well-known and highly respected auctioneer, as his partner.

The two men did not limit themselves to cattle, instead auctioning off every type of farm animal: sheep, pigs, rabbits, chickens, and on occasion even buffalo. Held indoors, the flourishing auctions soon outgrew their quarters, with participants spilling outside and vendors showing up to sell them dry goods and farm implements. The scene was set to create Maclin's first open-air market.

Maclin, quick as ever to recognize a good idea when he saw one, built booths for the vendors and charged them one dollar per day as rent. It was not long before just about everything imaginable was being offered for sale, ranging from clothing to produce to furniture to building materials.

The concept introduced a whole new element into the auction business, attracting people who were not necessarily interested in selling or buying livestock, but looking for a day of open-air fun and bargain hunting in a friendly, relaxed atmosphere. So popular did it become that the Maclin family expanded its auctions and the new open-air market idea into locations in San Jacinto in 1942 and Colton in 1949, where, along with the original operation in Ontario, they continue to thrive to this day.

As the enterprises grew, Maclin called upon his daughter Lillian and her husband, Don Nyberg, to assist him with the Chino Auction. Don Nyberg was a well-known leader in the dairy industry, running the Lucas Dairy Ranch, the largest in the area at the time, but he was willing to help out. Eventually the Nybergs turned over the operation to their daughters, Carol Ann and Mary Lou, and grandson, Brad Larsen, who would be responsible for the development of the operation into a highly successful business.

Brad, president and chief executive officer of the corporation, had worked at the open-air markets part time after school as a youngster and during the summer and holidays while attending the Army and Navy Academy in Carlsbad and later Cal Poly, Pomona. Although the company continues to be family held and run,

The original Chino Auction and Open Air Market is now Maclin Open Air Markets. Still on the same 40-acre site, the market sells thousands of items at bargain prices and features cattle, antique, and furniture auctions as well as children's rides, family entertainment, specialty restaurants, saloons, and beer gardens.

Brad and his wife, Liza Anne, and twin daughters, Amy Ann and Jennifer Leigh, currently are the only family members involved in its management. Brad's brother, Poul, has also assisted in the operation when he has not been either pursuing college degrees or building custom homes. Their mother, Carol Ann, handled the office operations until she retired in 1988.

Maclin's three auction and open-air markets employ more than 100 people, and their hundreds of vendors sell literally thousands of different items, from lingerie to hardware, some seconds or discontinued products, but almost all of them new, at prices reduced by lower operating costs and high-sales volume. They also feature goat, sheep, hog, horse, and cattle auctions and antique and furniture auctions, as well as children's rides and attractions, family entertainment, and specialty restaurants, saloons, and comfortable beer gardens.

The Chino Auction, which houses the firm's main office, is located at 7407 Riverside Drive, south of the Pomona Freeway off Euclid Avenue, and is open Tuesdays, Saturdays, and Sundays. San Jacinto Auction, at 789 North Lyon Avenue, south of the San Bernardino Freeway in San Jacinto in Riverside County, is open Saturdays, Sundays, and Wednesday nights during the summer. The Colton Auction, at 1902 West Valley Boulevard, north of the San Bernardino Freeway in Colton, is open Thursdays, Saturdays, and Sundays.

Brad Larsen, who sees the open-air markets as the most viable and attractive alternative for people seeking a fun change as well as huge savings when compared to enclosed malls and the drudgery usually associated with shopping for necessities, plans to expand Maclin in the years to come, adding other locations and eventually opening them seven days per week. Clean, well organized, and carefully monitored, Maclin Markets Inc.'s open-air markets continue to set the highest standards for an industry whose future they are helping to shape.

ONTARIO INTERNATIONAL AIRPORT

Ontario Municipal Airport in the 1930s consisted of two metal hangars and a dirt-strip runway on 34 acres.

When a Curtiss JN-4—a "Jenny"—soared skyward from a dirt airstrip called Latimer Field on July 25, 1923, in the first documented departure from an Ontario airport, it symbolized what perhaps was the most significant moment in the history of the area.

Latimer Field, named for Charles Latimer, who owned an orange-packing plant on the property and was instrumental in convincing the railroads to lease the land for an airport, was located between San Antonio and Mountain and the Southern and Union Pacific tracks. The cost to the airport was $145.65 per year.

Nine more planes soon joined the "Jenny," and the small fleet gave similarly small Ontario the arguable distinction of having more aircraft per capita than any city in the world. More important than that record were two aviators: Archie Delwood Mitchell, Ontario's city attorney and later a San Bernardino County superior court judge, credited with being the father of Ontario Airport, and Waldo Waterman, the most experienced of the early flyers, who was an instructor, me-

chanic, and aeronautical engineer. One flying enthusiast recalls heading for the airport, where "for two dollars, Waterman would take us up for a half-hour trip around the valley."

In about 1929 the airfield moved to the southwest corner of the present Ontario International Airport (ONT) site, where it became a weed patch until it was cleaned up

by American Legion Post No. 112 members one August night by the lights of automobiles parked around the perimeter.

Later, about a month before the stock market crash in 1929, Post No. 112 came forward again, this time borrowing funds from an Ontario bank to purchase the 30 acres that would eventually grow to today's 1,450-acre ONT. The Legionnaires were the forerunners of what in time would be a support organization called the Friends of the Airport. The new Ontario Airport functioned at a low level of activity until June 7, 1936, when an air show and dedication ceremonies were held. At that time, as the possibility of World War II became increasingly likely, the Ontario City Council began discussing an expansion of the facility for purposes of national defense.

Four years would pass, however, until voters approved a $150,000 bond issue, and a federal grant of

Ontario International Airport entered the jet age in the 1960s as flights scheduled for Los Angeles International were diverted to Ontario because of coastal fog. ONT's ability to accommodate the large jets (Convair 880s in the background) demonstrated that the airport could play a major role in Southern California aviation.

$351,000 was received for improvement of the runways, buildings, and grounds.

By 1942 Ontario Airport had two reinforced concrete runways. After Pearl Harbor, it was taken over by the federal government and became the Ontario Air Base. Throughout the war the airport was constantly busy, used for a variety of military purposes that would eventually change it into the Ontario Army Base for training with Lockheed's P-38 Lightning.

When the war ended, activity at the airport dropped dramatically until it was returned to the City of Ontario on September 30, 1947. By that time the airport had George Sanford as its manager and International Air Transportation Company as the air freight operation, the latter sparking the name change to Ontario International Airport.

On October 27, 1949, Western Airlines began the first scheduled airline service into ONT. The following year Northrop Aircraft Company moved there as a final delivery point for the F-89 Scorpion.

ONT is ranked as one of the 100 busiest airports in the world and is expected to serve 12 million passengers by the year 2000.

At the request of the Air National Guard, the first of three runway extensions was built in 1952 to accommodate its increasingly faster aircraft. That same year Lockheed established an aircraft overhaul base, and the Ontario City Council approved design and construction of the control tower. Then, in 1955, Bonanza Airlines became ONT's second air carrier with DC-3 service to Palm Springs, Blythe, and Phoenix.

The City of Los Angeles purchased ONT in 1967 for approximately $1.2 million and the agreement to develop the airport as needed. By 1972 airlines such as American, Continental, PSA (now USAir), and AirCal had been added, and ONT recorded its first one-million-passenger year. In 1979, 2 million passengers went through the airport, and extensions were being added to the terminal building rather than the runways.

Today Ontario International Airport is a full-service origin and destination airport with commercial jet service to every major city in the United States, as well as to many international destinations, including Mexico City, London, Paris, and Frankfurt. Its commercial airlines also now

Ontario International Airport serves 5 million passengers annually and accommodates 6,700 vehicles in its main and auxiliary parking lots.

include Alaska, Delta, Transworld (TWA), America West, Southwest, United, and Northwest, plus such commuter airlines as SkyWest and United Express.

ONT is a major air-freight hub for United Parcel Service and Federal Express. Other freight companies and most of the jet airlines also carry freight in and out of the airport.

Ranking as one of the 100 busiest airports in the world, ONT continues to grow, expecting its total of 5 million annual passengers in 1988 to reach 12 million by the year 2000. To handle that enormous increase, plans are under way to build a new, $250-million, 535,000-square-foot terminal that will be nine times the size of the present one and accommodate 36 aircraft and 10,000 automobiles.

That first symbolic flight by the Jenny from Latimer Field in 1923 foretold the reaching of heights for Ontario and the airport that even today are still being transcended.

PITTENGER-ALAIR INSURANCE SERVICES, INC.

In 1923, when young Vernon R. Pittenger left at the end of the day as a line worker at General Electric, he entered an entirely different world. Each evening, operating out of shared space in a real estate office at "B" Street and Laurel in Ontario, he became the owner and sole employee of his newly established insurance agency. It was the forerunner of Pittenger-Alair Insurance Services Inc., today recognized as one of the most successful and stable independent commercial and personal insurance agencies in the Inland Empire.

After about two years of unrelenting hard work, Pittenger could devote full time to his company and move into his own office above a department store at "B" Street and Euclid. Six months later he moved again, this time to 134 North Euclid, where he stayed until 1936, when he relocated to 116 North Euclid.

In 1947 Pittenger took in a partner, Gene L. Alair, now a retired U.S. Navy Reserve captain, then fresh out of the Navy after seven years of service. Alair would become a full partner in 1950, when the firm changed its name to Pittenger-Alair Agency.

Two more moves would follow, in 1956 to 602 North Euclid and in 1960 to a building at "F" Street and Laurel—a structure the partners purchased. The firm would not move

again until 1981, when it bought its present building on the corner of Euclid and "F" Street.

Leon R. Lott, current agency president, joined the company in 1971. Six years later the Jack George Agency merged into Pittenger-Alair. Other officers are Brian J. Rogers, vice-president, and Paula Goertz, secretary/treasurer. Producers include Gene L. Alair, Jack C. George, Michael F. Ryan, and Tim Zalaha.

Pittenger-Alair has a staff of 18 people whose average length of service to the company is about 11 years (Paula Goertz has been there 33 years), a record of employee stability and longevity that is also reflected in its long-term affiliations with such insurance carriers as Commercial Union (since 1925) and United States Fidelity & Guaranty (since 1939). Its major carriers also include Aetna Life &

Casualty, Fireman's Fund, Kemper, and Sequoia.

The agency, one of the earliest to automate rating, policy issuance, and all of its functions, has a state-of-the-art computer system to help service its clients.

Since its beginning Pittenger-Alair Insurance Services, Inc. has dedicated itself to a philosophy that has resulted in long retention of its customers: an unwavering commitment to provide close personal attention and dependable service to each account. It is old-fashioned, perhaps, in today's increasingly impersonal business world, but a policy few would dispute.

The 1990 staff of Pittenger-Alair Insurance Services, Inc., brings personal attention and service to each of its accounts.

UNION PACIFIC REALTY COMPANY

When Union Pacific Corporation acquired more than 2,000 acres of land in the Inland Empire in the late 1960s for future industrial development, it was looking ahead to making a major commitment to the still largely unwritten history of explosive economic growth of the area. It would link together once again the fortunes of the Inland Empire with Union Pacific, but this time with the corporation's land and development division, rather than the railroad that helped open up Southern California in the 1860s.

In 1986 UP's Upland Industries Corporation changed its name to Union Pacific Realty Company and moved its Los Angeles offices to an Ontario site. Taking 500 of the original prime 2,000 acres, which also include Fontana and Riverside, the

Strategically located two miles east of Ontario International Airport next to Interstate 15 and between Interstate 10 and California 60, Vintage Industrial Park is projected to be one of the largest and most important corporate environments in the area when completed.

firm began the development of Vintage Industrial Park in the southeast corner of Ontario, projected to be one of the largest and most important corporate environments in the area when completed.

Located next to the fast-flowing north-south Interstate 15 and between the Interstate 10 and California Route 60 freeways, with easy entrance to all three, Vintage Industrial Park is only about two miles east of Ontario International Airport and also offers railway service. These are factors critically attractive to companies seeking to establish distribution centers away from the congestion, gridlock traffic, and high land costs of the Los Angeles area. Additional advantages include a large and highly motivated labor force along with affordable housing, two increasingly rare components that still are available in western San Bernardino County.

Companies already operating at Vintage Industrial Park include Hyundai Motor America, which bought 35 acres and built a $21-mil-

Completed buildings within the Vintage Industrial Park have placed Union Pacific Realty Company among the top 25 industrial developers in the United States.

lion parts and distribution center, the largest Hyundai depot in the nation; Caterpillar Inc., with its 409,000-square-foot parts-distribution western headquarters; and American Honda, with a 480,000-square-foot distribution center. Other companies with distribution facilities at Vintage are Sears, Roebuck and Co., L.A. Gear, Reebok, 3M, and Tappan/Frigidaire.

Union Pacific Realty, pursuing its longtime strategy of shifting from a land management to a land and building development company, sells only about half of any particular property and uses the remainder for speculative or build-to-suit construction for sale or lease. Already its completed buildings at Vintage Industrial Park have placed the firm's Ontario regional office among the top 25 industrial developers in the United States.

Conscious of Ontario's rich wine-making heritage, Union Pacific Realty Company appropriately calls its development "Vintage" and has given the streets within it such names as "Champagne" and "Burgundy." It is a tribute that the early settlers would have appreciated.

GRABER OLIVE HOUSE

One hundred and fifty tons of olives per year may not be overwhelming production by agricultural statistics. But quality, not quantity, has been the rule at the Graber Olive House since 1894 and is a key ingredient in the success of this four-generation business in Ontario.

Founder Clifford C. Graber set the high standards at the very beginning when he broke all the rules of olive growing by ripening every olive on the tree—a time-consuming and expensive procedure that means that pickers must return to each tree as many as seven times.

The result, however, is an unusually flavorful gourmet olive that is famous worldwide. The olives may be purchased direct or as far away as Tokyo and are found in America's finest restaurants and specialty shops.

Cliff Graber arrived in Ontario from Clay City, Indiana, in 1892 with his brother, Charles. Then only 19, Graber began raising the fruit on a small-scale basis to sell with his other produce. In 1905 Clifford married Georgia Belle Noe, and the new Mrs. Graber was soon selling olives by the dipper from the olive vats.

Knowing that many customers would prefer olives uniformly sized, Cliff designed and built a wooden olive grader, the basic concept of which is still used to sort olives. Neighbors and friends worked with the family at harvest time.

Olive sales swelled around 1910. In addition to being sold fresh-cured direct from the vats, the olives were now being canned. Graber needed more land and in the 1920s moved his growing operation to Hemet in Riverside County, though processing, canning, and sales would remain in Ontario.

The cannery was enlarged in 1934, and nine years later Graber's two sons, Robert and William, took over the business in partnership with a brother-in-law. Cliff, however, remained active in the company until his death in 1955 at age 83.

Robert eventually emerged as sole owner and in 1963 moved the ranching operations to 75 acres of olive groves in the San Joaquin Valley, where it remains today.

Throughout the years the original Graber quality standard has never been compromised. To prevent bruising, a picker holds no more than three olives in his hand and deposits them in a padded bucket. The olives are never oxidized, and no artificial coloring is used.

Robert now serves as chairman of the board and his son, Clifford II, has become president; Robert's wife, Betty, is vice-president in charge of Graber's two gift shops; and young Clifford III, great-grandson of the founder, has enjoyed helping in the plant since the early age of three.

During the October-to-January processing period, Graber hires

Clifford C. Graber, founder.

about 60 workers and has given many Ontario students their first job. But by contrast, there are many long-term employees with one approaching 60 seasons with the company.

Now also a popular, year-round tourist stop, the Graber Olive House is a unique blend of old and new. At peak production, the plant pulsates with the vibrance of any modern factory. Yet, only yards away, turn-of-the-century structures built by the founder still stand strong, perhaps as a tribute to the heritage of Ontario's oldest existing business.

Robert D. Graber inspects a vat of olives in the processing room at Graber Olive House.

UNITED PARCEL SERVICE

Probably the thing most different about successful entrepreneurs is the ability to see beyond the boundaries of an existing opportunity in ways not evident to others. There are few better examples of that than the founding by a group of teenagers of what would become United Parcel Service, whose worldwide operations today include a major facility at Ontario International Airport.

Led by 19-year-old James E. Casey, the company borrowed $100 in 1907 to start a messenger service business in Seattle. Most available telephones then were public. People would use them to call a messenger service to hand carry their messages to their destinations. There was a need for a well-managed messenger company that would offer customers courtesy, reliability, and around-the-clock service.

Thus the American Messenger Company, a forerunner of United Parcel Service, was born. Its founders were determined to never make a promise they could not keep. Soon posters were tacked up next to every public telephone reading "Best Service, Lowest Rates," a

philosophy that continues today, nearly a century later, to guide UPS.

It would be six years before the U.S. Postal Service would introduce the parcel post system, but the fledgling company already had begun to focus on packages, delivering parcels from a local clothing store to its customers.

In 1913 the firm merged with a competitor, changing its name to Merchants Parcel Delivery, acquiring motorcycles and a Model T Ford. In 1919 the company was doing so well that it extended its operations to Oakland, California, where the name United Parcel Service was adopted. After expanding its retail service on the West Coast, UPS started service in New York City in 1930, and during the next 15 years

United Air Express, UPS' first foray into air service in February 1929, provided customers with service to and from major West Coast cities.

A vintage UPS package car meets the company's first 757 jet freighter. The aircraft is the only standard body jet freighter in production today. UPS operates or has on order 30 of the Boeing-built aircraft.

expanded to cities throughout the East and Midwest.

By the early 1950s it became clear that contract service to stores no longer had growth potential, and UPS decided to compete directly with the U.S. Postal Service by acquiring common-carrier rights to deliver packages. It would take more than three decades to fully accomplish, but in 1987 UPS became the first package delivery company in history to service every address in the United States. Today, with a combination of air and ground service, UPS provides the United States with the most broad-based coverage possible. UPS is the only private company to service every delivery address in the United States. It also has extended its operation internationally, and its air fleet serves more than 180 countries and territories.

United Parcel Service recently expanded its facilities adjacent to Ontario International Airport, is constructing a 500,000-square-foot combined air package sorting and ground delivery center on 160 acres, and relocated its aircraft to a 50-acre concrete ramp for loading and unloading. Among the primary beneficiaries of these improved services are Ontario and surrounding communities of the Inland Empire and Southern California.

SCHLOSSER FORGE COMPANY

When the Space Shuttle *Challenger* orbited the earth on its maiden voyage, each of the three engines that powered the craft in outer space contained more than 200 components forged by Schlosser Forge Company in Rancho Cucamonga. It was the kind of sky-reaching accomplishment that aptly symbolizes the entrepreneurship of Phillip D. Schlosser, a man who views the world as a place of unlimited opportunities, and the successful enterprise he founded.

Between serving in the U.S. Navy during World War II and the Korean War, Phil Schlosser graduated in 1951 from the University of Wisconsin with a degree in metallurgy. In 1954, after Korea, he started on the road that would lead him to the business independence he sought.

Like most entrepreneurs, he was never comfortable working for others. He also understood that

the more he learned about the complexities of the forging industry, the better able he would be to begin his own operation.

In a series of three-year stints, he worked for several major forge shops: Ladish Company in Cudahy, Wisconsin, as a process controller; Ladish's West Coast division in Vernon, California, as a metallurgist; Reisner Metals in Southgate, California, as chief metallurgist (where he worked on the Minuteman Missile program); Taylor Forge in the Chicago area as plant manager; and finally, Carlton Forge in Paramount, California, as general manager.

Phillip D. Schlosser and the small building in the middle of a Cucamonga grapevine where he founded Schlosser Forge Company in 1970.

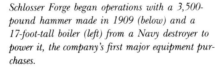

Schlosser Forge began operations with a 3,500-pound hammer made in 1909 (below) and a 17-foot-tall boiler (left) from a Navy destroyer to power it, the company's first major equipment purchases.

By 1970 he felt he was ready to go it alone and founded Schlosser Forge Company in a small building in the middle of a grape vineyard in Cucamonga, hauling in a 3,500-pound hammer made in 1909 and a 17-foot-tall boiler out of a Navy destroyer to power it. That same year he custom built a $17,000, 40-inch

Phil Schlosser represented manufacturing industries in the 1985 Rancho Cucamonga Founders' Day Parade, flanked by his grandsons, Eric Schlosser and Jeffrey Holguin. Phil's wife, Elaine, is driving and Danny Warner is in the front seat.

vertical ring mill and installed it on Christmas Day (a $2.5-million ring mill replaces it today). Using that relatively primitive equipment, he would successfully produce small runs for developmental engines for General Electric and Pratt & Whitney.

It had taken him until November 11, 1970, to get that first hammer operational, and, ignoring superstition, the company had opened for business on Friday, November 13. That night a Santa Ana wind roared through the valley and tore the doors off his new plant. His dismay soon turned to anger and a reaffirmed determination to let nothing stop him.

And nothing did. The family worked every day of the year for three years. Schlosser Forge Company then reached the point where real growth could begin. Schlosser then changed his role from doer to manager, spending the next three years training skilled people to take over the myriad of duties he and his family had been performing. As a result, the firm soon was up and going in the way envisioned by its

founder. In 1976 Schlosser Forge was named the Outstanding Small Business Manufacturer by the U.S. Small Business Administration.

It has been no easy task. Today there are only eight companies within the United States that manufacture seamless-contoured rolled rings and forgings for jet aircraft engines, missiles, and rockets, most of them large, publicly held corporations. But privately owned Schlosser Forge Company stands tall among them, deriving its competitive strength from a consistent emphasis on quality service, products, and technology at reasonable prices.

Since its beginnings in 1970, Schlosser Forge has grown from annual gross sales of $30,000 to a healthy $40 million-plus and employs more than 200 people. About 30 percent of its business is forgings for military aircraft, with the rest encompassing commercial aircraft, aerospace, and nuclear-power industries.

A team of highly trained specialists—designers, engineers, metallurgists, and plant personnel—works to tailor products precisely to customers' needs. They are backed by a computer-aided design and manufacturing system, computer-operated forging equipment, and state-of-the-art material-handling and testing operations. Forging itself is a superior method for critical parts, where gaining the full potential in strength and durability available from metals is essential.

Because of their specific metallurgical properties, high-grade copper, stainless steel, iron- and nickel-base high-temperature alloys, aluminum, magnesium, molybdenum, titanium, and titanium alloys are used.

Still expanding, the Schlosser Forge Company continues as a family-operated enterprise, with Jeff Schlosser as president.

Phil Schlosser, who was elected Rancho Cucamonga's second mayor in 1980 and served on the city council from the time the city was incorporated in 1977 until 1982, has since gone on to new challenges. He now runs a 7,500-acre ranch with 500 head of cattle in central Oregon and, ever the entrepreneur, has also successfully founded Schlosser Casting Company, a wholly owned investment casting subsidiary of Schlosser Forge in Redmond, Oregon.

His astute business vision, coupled with his civic and community leadership, has become an integral part of the ongoing history of the Inland Empire.

Today sophisticated equipment, such as this $2.5-million, computer-controlled ring mill, and highly trained specialists work to tailor products precisely to customers' needs.

THE CITY OF ONTARIO

Since its founding as a model colony by the Chaffey brothers in 1882, Ontario has always understood the importance of cherishing the priceless legacy that makes it distinctive among other communities in the Inland Empire. And nowhere has that awareness been more apparent than in the consistent pattern of enlightened leadership that has shaped it into the hugely successful industrial and commercial center it is today.

In a state that was once the nation's last frontier, some say California now offers dwindling opportunities to turn dreams into reality. But Ontario continues to beckon with many of the same attractions that drew the early pioneers westward to it in the first place: good planning, reasonably priced open land, potential for economic growth, a pleasant place to live and raise a family, and perhaps most important of all, the exciting sense of being on the edge of a future still in the making.

But there are more advantages—the kinds of things that could not be perceived by the Ontario colony's settlers in the late 1800s. Things such as the city's location at the hub of a transportation network of freeways, railroads, and Ontario International Airport that allows industries and businesses unparalleled access to their markets; a large skilled and unskilled labor force seeking work close to home that will end their long commuting to jobs elsewhere and thus improve the quality of their lives; plenty of affordable housing; excellent hospitals; good schools and nearby colleges; a booming hospitality industry of hotels, motels, restaurants, and catering services; a fine library, a museum, and a growing reputation as a cultural center; well-kept parks and organized recreation programs; efficient police and fire departments; and a unique distribution center designated as a foreign trade zone.

Overseeing and giving direction to Ontario's present and future growth is a supportive city government and administration, operating since 1979 out of a handsome and modern civic center that employs more than 1,000 people—a far cry from December 23,

American Trading's Empire Tower in Ontario.

1891, when Ontario was incorporated and its first officials were appointed.

Known as the board of trustees, the forerunner of what later would become an elected council, its eight officers were D.T. Jones (mayor), J.P. Ensley, W.T. Randall, J.P. Robertson (treasurer), E. Du Bois (city clerk), and L.J.E. Tyler (marshal), A.E. Tracy, and D.S. Cochran. They were sworn in by George R. Holbrook, justice of the peace.

Showing the same dynamic leadership that marks it today, the city by 1896 could boast progress that was little short of phenomenal. Although it was only 14 years old, it already had electric lights and power, an electric railway, a sewer system, a college, five public schools, two kindergartens, a library, six churches, two banks, two newspapers, two hotels, a large fruit-canning plant, a fruit-drying plant, fruit packinghouses, two transcontinental railroads, a narrow-gauge railroad to Chino, fraternal societies, and several sports clubs. And, of course, there was also its most famous attribute, Euclid

Palmbrook at Ontario.

Avenue, a magnificent 200-foot-wide, eight-mile-long boulevard designed by the Chaffeys and still the city's centerpiece. A living link with those times survives today in the world-renowned Graber Olive House, founded in 1894 by Clifford C. Graber, which is Ontario's oldest existing business.

As the years passed Ontario continued to grow and prosper while it sought to improve every crucial area that affected the quality of its life. In 1960, for example, the city changed the procedure under which the mayor was appointed by the council members so that its residents could have a greater say in choosing their leadership by voting directly for who would hold that office. It was a move that would also

result in the city clerk becoming an elected position.

That attention to the concerns of its citizens and the kind of government that depends more on being a partnership rather than an autocratic system has maintained the advanced and balanced perception in the eyes of others that the city has enjoyed from the beginning. How successful it has been is best illustrated by examining some of the major activities currently under way or being planned for the future.

An important catalyst and probably the largest contributor to Ontario's surging growth is the Ontario International Airport (ONT), which has helped attract such major developments as Chevron Land and Development Company's The Ontario

E.G. Maramore bought land from Chaffey Trust on November 23, 1887. He purchased block 17, lots 5 and 6. The grocery store was not on the property when he purchased it. Photo circa 1900

Center, Union Pacific Realty Company's Vintage Industrial Park, the Sickels Group's Centerlake Business Park, and the California Commerce Center with its foreign trade zone.

The foreign trade zone status is particularly appealing to companies engaged in international trade and importing. The largest privately owned such operation in the nation, the center technically is U.S. customs territory, and while materials are within it, they are not subject to a customs bond or U.S. duty or excise tax. When goods are directly exported out of the zone, no duty is paid, and when transferred into customs territory, only minimal amounts of duty are imposed.

A future project being considered by the city also relates to the presence of the busy and soon-to-be-expanded airport. It would see the construction of a convention/trade-show facility, probably located close to the area's airport-related hotels to take advantage of the airport's proximity and high-volume business traffic.

While the industrial, commercial, and residential growth of the 120,000-population city continues to boom, Ontario's downtown, like those of many other of California's older communities, has been largely eclipsed by the activity in the undeveloped portions of the city. Consequently, it has been created as a redevelopment project area to revitalize both it and East Holt Boulevard by determining strategies and policies to restore the identity and self-image of downtown as Ontario's historic center.

Some of it has already begun, with an 11-acre Ontario Village shopping center and efforts to refurbish and attract additional retail specialty stores, restaurants, and professional offices, all of which are expected to inject new life into downtown as part of the city's ambitious plans for the future.

Characteristically, the city is combining its legacy of practical and forward thinking with a deep regard for the preservation of its historical roots. Already the community's downtown area also features a museum, housed since 1979 in a handsome Spanish-Mediterranean-style building that had served for 42 years as the Ontario City Hall. The museum, which features history and art wings, is a part of the community's cultural offerings that include performing-arts shows and other special events held at the restored Gardiner W. Spring Auditorium, built in 1939 on the Euclid Avenue

campus of Chaffey High School. The Ontario City Library, today located in its own building adjacent to the Civic Center, has also been an intrinsic element of downtown since it was first founded with a $40 donation in the now razed Holt Adobe in 1885.

The Ontario Redevelopment Agency, acutely aware of the importance of historic preservation when at all feasible, now owns three buildings that it is studying for the possibility of renovation and reuse. These are the Gallery Theater, built as a church in 1908 and later used for theater-in-the-round performances; the Fallis House, constructed in about 1900 by William B. Fallis, owner of what was one of Ontario's major department stores for many

BELOW and FACING: Two views of Euclid Avenue, a two-lane avenue eight miles long, which was laid out by George and William Chaffey in 1882. Photo circa 1900

years; and the Casa Bianca Hotel, built in 1915 when it was hailed as one of the finest such establishments in Southern California.

In the midst of Ontario's commercial development, residential needs are also receiving high priority, with two-phase, 410-acre Creekside Village. Located at the base of the San Gabriel Mountains and adjacent to a large agricultural region known primarily for its dairy farming, vineyards, and row crops, it is a planned community of 2,574 single-family detached and attached units and multifamily units in a recreation-oriented environment complete with open-space greenbelts and a network of pedestrian/bicycle paths connecting the east and west villages.

The project also offers an eight-acre lake and several activity centers, including tennis courts, spas, and swimming pools, as well as an elementary school, neighborhood service and retail outlets, and professional offices.

The city's recreation and parks system is another operation that contributes to Ontario's sense of community. With 24 parks encompassing more than 300 acres, including John Galvin Park, which, at 42 acres, is the largest, the system has 6 community centers, 6 neighborhood swimming pools, 12 lighted athletic fields, a gymnasium, a horse show ring, and a major-league-size baseball field.

Public safety, administered by the Ontario Police Department and the Ontario Fire Department, has come a long way since the city's early beginnings when, according to one source, "There was a marshal during the day and a night watchman after sunset. There were no police cars, no radio—nothing but a flashlight and a sharp tongue." And the fire department, which was not organized until 1905, consisted of a handful of volunteer citizens. Today the police department is one of the most efficient and effective in the area, and its state-of-the-art facilities include two helicopters and a canine unit. The fire department, long since staffed by professionals, has seven strategically located stations and an outstanding paramedic program.

Working closely with the city and sharing its goals for the future is the Ontario Chamber of Commerce and its more than 1,200 members, another example of the teamwork and pursuit of a common purpose that has hallmarked the community for more than a century.

In 1957, when Ontario celebrated the 75th anniversary of its founding, the prime minister of the Province of Ontario in Canada, after which the city was named by George Chaffey, wrote: "The great irrigation projects that have developed the semiarid land in the vicinity of your city show the great and beneficial results that follow when men's ingenuity is used for creative development."

He was referring to engineer Chaffey's remarkable feat of supplying water to the early residents of Ontario Model Colony and his development of the first use of hydroelectric power on the Pacific slope. But his real salute was to the careful, master-planned growth that Chaffey's latter-day successors have continued to cherish.

PILGRIM PLACE

Pilgrim Place celebrates its 75th anniversary in 1990 with a continuing vigor and joyfulness that belie its description as a retirement community.

Composed of former professional church workers living out their days in a positive atmosphere, this center has been touching the surrounding communities in a special way from its quiet streets and pleasant gardens in Claremont.

Residents sponsor the Pilgrim Festival, a unique two-day event held each November that looks and sounds much like a seventeenth-century country fair and carnival and annually attracts more than 10,000 people. It has two primary purposes: to raise funds for the residents' emergency health fund and to provide a fun-filled event for all ages. Assisted by more than 700 volunteers, the 325 residents (most dressed in Pilgrim costumes) staff the event that they plan and work tirelessly on together throughout the year.

Founded in 1915 by a dozen

The Sixth Street entrance to Pilgrim Place, with Porter Hall in the background. This nonprofit religious and cultural center offers housing and health services for retired church professionals.

Congregationalists as a residence for missionaries and their children on furlough, Claremont Missionary Home was the beginning of what would later become Pilgrim Place in 1924. Although there were many others, the main energy for the development of the home would come from four prominent families: the Porters, Blaisdells, Nortons, and Renwicks. Helen Renwick of Claremont donated five lots on what today is the Scripps College campus and later added a third cottage to the two given by the Porters.

Claremont Missionary Home eventually would outgrow its quarters and move to its present location on 20 acres at Sixth Street and Berkeley Avenue, where it was renamed Pilgrim Place and changed its purpose toward what it is now: a

The Pilgrim Festival, a fun-filled event to raise funds for the residents' emergency health fund, is held each November. Shown here are hundreds of people watching the historical pageant. The canopies cover two dozen bazaar booths, where a variety of arts and crafts along with other items are sold.

community serving retired missionaries, ministers, and other church workers, as well as their spouses, who have given the major proportion of their careers (at least 20 years) in salaried professional Christian employment. Presently Pilgrim Place has a long waiting list extending into the next century.

Through their own efforts and the generous support of a great many friends, Pilgrims have built a unique complex that not only boasts its own modern Health Services Center, but offers its residents a plethora of stimulating cultural and arts and crafts activities housed in handsome and functional facilities.

Although governed by a volunteer board of directors (one-fourth of whom are residents), Pilgrim Place is democratically self-governed by its own residents through their Town Meeting. Pilgrim Place is a vibrant community of involved and fulfilled people who essentially view their lives there as an extension of their previous careers as dedicated Christian workers. They personify Tennyson's observation: "'Tis not too late to seek a newer world; Tho' much is taken, much abides."

BOMATIC, INC.

The Bomatic, Inc., BMI plant No. 2, located at 2181 East Francis Street in Ontario, has 43,000 square feet of manufacturing, warehouse, sales, and shipping offices. Bomatic, Inc., has occupied the building since August 1987

When Borge Hestehave was growing up in Elsinore in German-occupied Denmark, he already knew what he wanted—to own his own business. In time he would succeed dramatically, founding Bomatic, Inc., a nationally recognized industrial blow-molding design and manufacturing company in Ontario. Although the route to his goal would be circuitous, he would never falter on his way to achieving it.

Following graduation from Copenhagen University in 1948 with a degree in mechanical engineering, Borge was offered an opportunity by a firm to start a factory in Santiago, Chile, to make toothpaste tubes. A level of opportunity and challenge available to few young men beginning their careers, it was a forecast of his future achievements.

Four years later, in 1956, Borge; his wife, Marianne; their son, Kjeld; and infant daughter, Judy, left for the United States. He worked as a tool and die maker in Los Angeles and as a plant engineer for Flintkote Paper Company in Vernon before joining Sunland Molded Products, a division of Latchford Glass, and then Kerr Plastics as plant manager.

He was almost ready to go out on his own, but first there would be a partnership in 1962 with Leonard Robinson, owner of Magic-Cup Corporation in Berkeley. During the next four years the team would invent and patent the now widely used injection blow-molding machine.

His reputation firmly established in the blow-molding industry, Hestehave went to Trans-Container in Upland as plant manager, his final move before founding Bomatic, Inc., in 1969 in a partnership with veteran mold-maker and good friend Henry A. Myers.

Starting in a leased 2,000-square-foot building in Ontario, the firm struggled to get a foothold in the competitive blow-molding business. By 1971 Bomatic was able to move to a 5,000-square-foot facility, and four years later it bought out Technical Plastics. Today a sales division of Bomatic named Totem Plastics, it markets the firm's gasoline, kerosene, and water containers.

In recent years Bomatic has expanded into two large, modern plants, one also housing corporate headquarters at 1841 East Acacia Street and the other sales headquarters at 2181 East Francis Street, both in Ontario. Using the latest technology and the most advanced equipment, the company provides full-service designing and engineering, mold-making, and product production for customers nationwide. Employing 100 people, the family-owned and -controlled firm continues to grow under the leadership of Borge Hestehave, board chairman; his son, Kjeld, president; his wife, Marianne, vice-president; and daughter, Judy, in sales and marketing.

It has been a long journey from Denmark, but for Borge Hestehave it is the fulfillment of a dream that he never doubted would be realized.

Located at 1841 East Acacia Street in Ontario, Bomatic, Inc., has been at its headquarters, a 31,500-square-foot manufacturing, moldshop, warehouse, and office facility, since January 1978.

HMC GROUP
(formerly HMC ARCHITECTS, INC.)

In 1940, when architect Jay Dewey Harnish opened a small office on "B" Street just east of Euclid Avenue in Ontario, it probably would have seemed farfetched to predict that he was starting a firm that one day would earn a national reputation for its work in health care, education, and government projects. The local area was still a relatively sleepy agricultural community, and the nation was edging closer to war—neither were good omens for a professional future. But Harnish saw it differently.

From 1941 to 1945 he concentrated his efforts on the design of military housing in San Bernardino, Colton, Redlands, and Barstow, laying the foundation for the highly specialized practice in institutional work that he correctly anticipated would come with peacetime.

Harnish, who had moved to Upland in 1910 with his parents, attended local schools and later served in France during World War I. He earned his degree in architecture from the University of California, Berkeley and, following a brief period working in San Francisco,

joined the firm of York and Sawyer in New York. It was there he was introduced to design for hospital projects, the base on which he would build his career.

Eventually he returned to Southern California, where he designed sets for Metro-Goldwyn-Mayer and RKO Studios before becoming associated with the San Bernardino firm of DeWitt-Mitchem, then heavily involved with the Works Progress Administration (WPA). As economic conditions improved and his architectural background broadened, Harnish felt ready to establish his own practice.

Soon he had architectural contracts at San Bernardino County General Hospital, the beginning of

a relationship that would extend for many years and establish a reputation for client longevity that continues today with a record that includes 49 years of service to San Antonio Community Hospital, Upland; 37 years to Pomona Valley Hospital Medical Center; 25 years to Kaiser Permanente; 20 years to Parkview Community Hospital, Riverside; and 18 years to Western Medical Center, Santa Ana.

In 1960 Jack Causey and M.C. Morgan joined him in Ontario, creating the partnership known as Harnish, Morgan, and Causey until 1978, when it became HMC Architects.

Over its 50 years of existence the firm has developed plans for more than 61 schools locally and

HMC Group's client longevity is evident in projects such as San Antonio Community Hospital in Upland (right), which goes back 49 years. The hospital continues to grow as shown in the architect's renderings (below and below right) of future expansion.

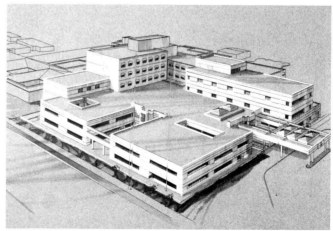

throughout Southern California and is the campus architect for California State University, San Bernardino. In Ontario, HMC's contributions to the skyline include the Ontario Public Library, the Ontario Post Office, the Southern California Edison office building, the General Electric Portable Appliances Center, and the Lockheed Engineering office building. At Ontario International Airport, it has designed the General Electric Jet Test Facility and the Lockheed Aircraft Services administration facility, as well as the architectural designs for the airport's first terminal building in 1946 and some of the subsequent additions.

During the early 1970s the firm's reputation for excellence grew significantly outside the immediate area when it completed projects for Hoag Memorial Hospital in Newport Beach, Downey Community Hospital in Downey, Presbyterian Intercommunity Hospital in Whittier, Desert Hospital in Palm Springs, and a variety of government and commercial assignments.

Harnish retired in 1978, when his associates took on three new partners, James Chase, Kenneth Taylor, and Walter Siegl. Today Chase is president and chief executive officer and manages the company, with principals Siegl as executive vice-president, Donal

Endsley as vice-president, and two senior associates, James Gilliam and Robert Kain, who were promoted to principals February 1, 1990.

Ongoing changes in the health care industry have altered the profile of HMC's diverse portfolio of projects. These range from the impressive 815,000-square-foot medical center for Kaiser Permanente in Baldwin Park to the unique Moreno Valley Medical Mall, the 28-bed Bear Valley Hospital, and the striking architecture of the chapel at Torrance's Little Company of Mary Hospital.

HMC's services have grown to include interior design, master planning, and recently, electrical and mechanical engineering. Computer-aided drafting and design (CADD) was added in 1985.

Two major examples of the firm's technical expertise are a direct heritage of Harnish's development of a highly specialized service. These are the cogeneration power plant completed in 1984 at St. Luke Hospital in Pasadena that generates electrical power for the acute care facility and sells back surplus power to the utility company, and, in 1985, the four-story Foothill Communities Law and Justice Center in Rancho Cucamonga, the world's largest structure to feature the unique structural

design of base isolation, isolating the building from ground motion by designing seismic bearings in its underground support system to withstand major earthquakes.

While the company he founded has made and continues to make important contributions to the world of architecture, Harnish can also take pride in his own involvement in the activities of the place where it all began—Ontario. Active in the Ontario Chamber of Commerce and its president in 1939-1940, he was a leading member of the chamber's Aviation Committee, which was instrumental in the city's purchase of the first segment of land to create Ontario International Airport. His wife, Jerene Appleby Harnish, has made a mark in the community as the former owner of the Ontario *Daily Report* and as a civic leader.

A new HMC headquarters building is planned to open in 1990 to coincide with the firm's 50th anniversary, a celebration that is also a noteworthy reflection of Jay Dewey Harnish's personal as well as corporate contribution to the growth of Ontario.

LEFT: Foothill Communities Law and Justice Center is a stunning example of HMC's technical expertise.

BELOW: A model of the Ontario-Montclair Elementary School No. 34.

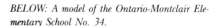
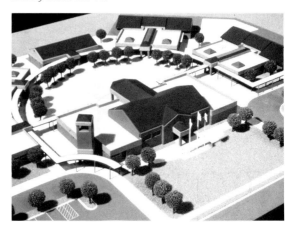

OLD ENGLISH RANCHO

Driving along Mission Boulevard just south of Ontario International Airport, a casual observer may fleetingly wonder about the unexpected rural scene of horses and white corrals in the midst of a growing encirclement of industrial buildings. What few realize is that they are looking at one of the largest and most successful thoroughbred racehorse breeding ranches in California.

It all began in 1939, when Ellwood B. Johnston, who had come west from Philadelphia at age 14 and subsequently made his fortune in a bakery business, bought a racehorse called English Harry. The horse won its very first race, and Johnston was hooked. Soon he built his own stable and bought a stallion named Old English. The stallion was another winner and the first of many horses Johnston would purchase from moviemaker Louis B. Mayer, a leading breeder.

Meanwhile, Johnston and Ted Tepper, his bakery business partner, acquired 37 acres on Riverside Drive in Chino to start their own breeding farm, which they named after Old English. Among others, they produced a two-year-old filly, Ruth Lily. She was their first homebred stakes winner and one of the best in her class in the nation.

In 1957 Johnston's son, Ellwood W. "Bud" Johnston, graduated from college, got married, and took over the running of the ranch, which by then had expanded to an additional 100 acres in Corona. The elder Johnston sold his bakery in 1960, and three years later he and his son, along with their wives, Betty and Judy, formed a partnership to concentrate on the horse business on 120 acres that the elder Johnston had bought in 1955 in Ontario, the present site of Old English Rancho.

Their success was phenomenal. For two years running, the ranch was named the leading breeder of stake horses in the United States, an accomplishment accompanied by being the leading breeder in California for 13 of the past 18 years. Today the ranch's trophy rooms are filled to overflowing.

Old English Rancho has two racing stables of 20 horses each, one in Northern California and the other in Southern California. It also has a 370-acre ranch in Sanger, outside of Fresno, where the entire operation will move within the next two or three years, fulfilling a plan originally made 25 years ago, when the elder Johnston thought the current rapid industrial growth of Ontario would begin sooner than it did.

Bud Johnston, now president of Old English Rancho, will then develop the land for industrial purposes, but hopes to place on it an appropriate memorial to the ranch's significant contributions to the history of Ontario and thoroughbred horse racing over the years. It will help future generations to recall the legacy of a community rooted deeply in a rural past.

Old English Rancho in the Winner's Circle. Willie Shoemaker (third from left) rode King's Mistake to victory in the 1957 Santa Maria Handicap. Attending the victory celebration (from left) were Betty Johnston, Judy Johnston, E.W. "Bud" Johnston, A.T. Doyle, and E.B. Johnston.

THE INLAND VALLEY DAILY BULLETIN

In 1910 Ontario was basically an agricultural community with a population of only 4,274, an unlikely place to start a daily newspaper. Editor Fred E. Uholz thought otherwise. On September 12 of that year he launched the *Daily Republican,* sending word to potential advertisers that "if they knew how we have been besieged to start a daily, they would at least realize what advertising in such a paper is worth."

Even including nearby Upland and its minuscule population of 2,384 in his circulation projection, Uholz seemed to be taking an unrealistic gamble. The communities already were supporting a weekly newspaper, *The Record Observer.* But history was to prove him right. Although in 1912 Uholz sold the paper to two brothers, Crombie and H.L. Allen, he had founded what was to become today's highly successful newspaper, *The Inland Valley Daily Bulletin.*

Named *The Daily Report* by the Allens, it would be published by them until 1930, when they sold it to Frank and Jerene Appleby. When Frank died in 1936, his widow, Jerene (later Jerene Appleby Harnish), took over direction of the newspaper and ran it for the next quarter-century.

In April 1965 Jerene Harnish sold *The Daily Report* to the Progress Publishing Company in Pomona, a firm owned by A.T. Richardson and his son, Charles T. Richardson, who became the new publisher. The Richardsons initiated a $600,000 expansion program for a new pressroom with a larger press and the remodeling of existing facilities.

Two years later *The Daily Report,* the *Pomona Progress Bulletin,* and six area weekly newspapers were purchased by the Donrey Media Group, whose founder, Donald W. Reynolds, became the publisher.

The Daily Report converted from afternoon to morning delivery in

Since its establishment in 1910, The Inland Valley Daily Bulletin *has served as the number-one source of local and national news for Ontario and its surrounding communities. Through the years the newspaper has undergone various format changes, including a conversion from evening to morning publication.*

The Inland Valley Daily Bulletin's *state-of-the-art offset presses, located at 2041 East Fourth Street, enable the newspaper to keep pace with the fast-growing community it serves.*

July 1986 and in October of that year moved from its Ontario home of more than 50 years on "B" Street to its present state-of-the-art, $25-million, 88,000-square-foot facility on Fourth Street. In May 1987 the *Progress Bulletin* in Pomona began printing its newspaper on *The Daily Report's* offset presses, capable of turning out 224 pages—many with full-color capabilities—and up to 50,000 copies per hour. The two newspapers then combined their Saturday and Sunday editions into one publication. *The Inland Valley Daily Bulletin* now serves the Inland Valley communities of Ontario, Chino, Rancho Cucamonga, Montclair, Claremont, Upland, Pomona, San Dimas, La Verne, Diamond Bar, Mt. Baldy, Guasti, and Fontana.

Fred Uholz' vision may have seemed blurred to some back in 1910, but in reality it was as well focused as it is today.

COVINGTON & CROWE

When an accomplished young lawyer, Samuel P. Crowe, and a highly regarded older colleague, Maurice G. Covington, decided to form a partnership in Ontario in 1967, they were creating what was destined to become one of the area's most comprehensive and successful law firms, emphasizing business, real estate, and governmental affairs.

Covington had been a partner in the prestigious law firm of Flint & MacKay prior to affiliating with Crowe. He brought with him the kind of professional recognition and respect that would be the hallmark of the firm thereafter.

Born in Redlands, Covington graduated from Pomona College with a B.A. degree in 1931 and from Harvard Law School with an LL.B. degree in 1934, the same year he was admitted to the bar. Today he continues to be widely known for his expertise in estate planning, probate, and trust administration.

Crowe, a native of Ashville, Alabama, had already established his own law practice, Crowe, Bailin, Gladson, in Ontario when he and Covington decided to form the firm of Covington & Crowe. His contribution to the partnership was a youthful enthusiasm rooted in a sound knowledge of the legal profession and law.

Crowe received a bachelor's degree from the University of California at Los Angeles in 1957 and a J.D. degree from the University of Southern California in 1960. A certified specialist in taxation law, Crowe's areas of expertise include corporations, partnerships, estate planning, and governmental law. Currently, he is city attorney for Ontario and previously has served in that capacity for the city of Rancho Cucamonga.

An active leader in community affairs, Crowe was an Ontario city councilperson from 1964 to 1972 and has been a member of the Ontario City Planning Commission; the Airport Commission, Ontario International Airport; and the Ontario Community Hospital Advisory Board.

When the firm of Covington & Crowe was founded in 1967, three additional lawyers, George W. Porter, Harold A. Bailin (who died in 1988), and Robert E. Dougherty, also brought their various areas of expertise and professional reputations to the fledgling practice.

Porter, who specializes in criminal defense and business litigation, recently has been named to the 1989-1990 edition of "The Best Lawyers in America," an extraordinary honor bestowed upon him by nomination of his peers.

Born in Manila, Philippine Islands, Porter earned his B.A. degree at the University of Redlands in 1952 and a J.D. degree at the University of California at Berkeley in 1958. A certified specialist in criminal law, he is a member and former president of the Western San Bernardino County and San Bernardino County Bar associations.

Dougherty, born in Honolulu, Hawaii, received his B.S. degree and, in 1967, a J.D. degree from the University of California at Los Angeles. Specializing in municipal law and business litigation, he is assistant city attorney for Ontario and former city attorney for Rancho Cucamonga.

Three other members of the firm have earned particular recognition for their noteworthy accomplishments in their fields: Donald G. Haslam, who received his B.A. degree from the University of California at Berkeley and is a 1967 graduate of UCB's Boalt Hall School of Law, specializing in divorce law; Robert F. Schauer, who earned a B.A. degree and in 1970, a J.D. degree from the University of California, Davis, specializing in construction litigation; and Edward A. Hopson, a former assistant city attorney for Rancho Cucamonga, who received a B.A. degree from Pomona College and, in 1972, a J.D. degree from the University of Southern California, specializing in real estate law.

Covington & Crowe today has 27 attorneys. An advocate of hiring women, the firm is particularly proud that six of its lawyers, including two partners, are female.

While offering a full range of legal services, the firm also provides specialized services in the areas of business, real estate, governmental affairs, criminal defense, bankruptcy, probate, estate planning and trusts, domestic relations, personal injury, and litigation. In addition, the firm is one of the few in the area that offers legal services in pension plan administration and profit sharing.

Because of its highly rated track record of professional competence and success, Covington & Crowe counts many of the major businesses, industries, professional firms, and banks in the Inland Empire among its large and growing list of corporate, municipal, and individual clients.

Occupying 20,000 square feet on the recently remodeled top floor of its own building at 1131 West Sixth Street in Ontario, the law firm has established an enviable reputation for dependability, integrity, and the ability to provide its clients with close, personal attention. It also provides personnel who are multilingual to serve clients as needed.

Covington & Crowe's place in the history of Ontario springs from the longtime active leadership involvement of its principals in the growing community's affairs, a commitment that is helping to shape the kind of future first envisioned for it by the early settlers seeking a new and better life in a new land.

San Antonio Creek provided water for the early colonies of Ontario and Pomona and was a quiet retreat for picnics in the summer. However, until the construction of San Antonio Dam in the 1950s, winter often found the towns flooded by the rain-swollen stream. Courtesy, Ontario City Library, Model Colony History Room

Patrons

The following individuals, companies, and organizations have made a valuable commitment to the quality of this publication. Windsor Publications and the Ontario Chamber of Commerce gratefully acknowledge their participation in *Ontario: The Model Colony*.

Bob & Ed's Glass*
Bomatic, Inc.*
California Commerce Center at Ontario*
California Occupational Medical Group*
Chino Valley Bank*
Mark Christopher Chevrolet*
The City of Ontario*
Covington & Crowe*
Daisy Wheel Ribbon Co., Inc.*

Glenn B. Dorning Inc.*
Employment Training Agency of the West End*
First American Title Insurance Company*
Graber Olive House*
HMC (formerly HMC Architects, Inc.) Group*
The Inland Valley Daily Bulletin*
Kawaco Inc.*
K mart Corporation
Lockheed Aircraft Service Company*
Loud Engineering and Manufacturing, Inc.*
Maclin Markets Inc.*
Mitsubishi Cement Corporation*
Monsanto Company
Old English Rancho*
The Ontario Center*

Ontario International Airport*
Pilgrim Place*
Pittenger-Alair Insurance Services, Inc.*
Pomona Die Casting Corp.*
San Antonio Orchard Company*
Schlosser Forge Company*
Shervington Hoskins & Co.
Southwest Concrete Products*
Structural Fibers
Transamerican Plastics Corporation*
Union Pacific Realty Company*
United Parcel Service*

*Partners in Progress of *Ontario: The Model Colony*. The histories of these companies and organizations appear in Chapter Seven, beginning on page 123.

Bibliography

Alexander, J.A. *The Life of George Chaffey: A Story of Irrigation Beginning in California and Australia.* Melbourne: Macmillan and Co. Ltd., 1928.

A Short Pictorial History of Ontario International Airport. Ontario International Airport, 1986.

Austen, Ruth. *Virginia Dare: Legend of the World's Largest Winery.* Unpublished manuscript, copyright 1983.

Beattie, George William and Helen Pruitt Beattie. *Heritage of the Valley: San Bernardino's First Century.* Pasadena: San Pasqual Press, 1939.

————. *Heritage of the Valley.* Oakland: Biobooks, 1951.

Bicentennial Salute: An Historical Review of Ontario and Our Nation—1776 to 1976. Ontario: Ontario Bicentennial Commission, 1976.

Black, Esther Boulton. *Rancho Cucamonga and Doña Merced.* Redlands: San Bernardino County Museum Association, 1975.

————. *Stories of Old Upland.* Upland: Chaffey Communities Cultural Center, 1979.

Bolton, Eugene. *Anza's California Expeditions.* Vols. I, II, and IV. Berkeley: University of California Press, 1930.

Brown, John Jr. and James Boyd. *History of San Bernardino and Riverside Counties.* Vol. I. Chicago: Lewis Publishing Co., 1922.

Burke, James *Connections.* Toronto: Little, Brown and Company, 1978.

Chapman, Charles Edward. *The Founding of Spanish California: The Northwest Expansion of New Spain, 1687-1783.* New York: Octagon Books, 1973.

Conley, Bernice Bedford. *Dreamers and Dwellers: Ontario and Neighbors.* Ontario: Stump Printing Services, 1982.

Cowan, Robert G. *Ranchos of California: A List of Spanish Concessions, 1775-1822; Mexican Land Grants, 1822-1846.* Fresno, California: Academy Library Guild, 1956.

————. *Floods of the Past: An Assemblage of Documentary Observations With Particular Reference to the San Bernardino Valley and Environs.* W. A. Sidler, compiler. San Bernardino County Flood Control District, 1957, expanded 1972.

————. *Geological Excursions in Southern California.* Wilfred A. Elders for the Geological Society of America, Cordilleran Section Meeting, University of California, Riverside, Campus Museum Contributions No. 1. Riverside: Unniversity of California, Riverside, 1971.

————. *Geology of Southern California.* Bulletin 170, Vol. I. Fresno: Division of Mines, State of California Department of Natural Resources, 1954.

————. *Handbook of North American Indians.* William C. Sturtevant, general editor.

Vol. 8, *California.* Robert F. Heizer, volume editor. Washington D.C.: Smithsonian Institute, 1978.

————. *Indians of Los Angeles County: Hugo Reid's Letters of 1852.* Robert F. Heizer, editor/compiler. Southwest Museum Papers, No. 21. Los Angeles: Southwest Museum, 1968.

Historical Essays by students of the Upland Elementary Schools. Upland Public Library, 1931.

Hofer, James D. *Cucamonga Wines and Vines: A History of the Cucamonga Pioneer Vineyard Association.* Master's thesis, Claremont Graduate School, 1983.

Ingersoll, Luther A. *Ingersoll's Century Annals of San Bernardino County 1769-1904.* Los Angeles: L.A. Ingersoll, 1904.

Knapp, Joseph G. *The Rise of American Cooperative Enterprise: 1620-1920.* Danville, Illinois: The Interstate Printers and Publishers, Inc., 1969.

Lawton, Harry and Lewis G. Weathers. "The Origins of Citrus Research in California." *The Citrus Industry, Volume V: Crop Protection, Postharvest Technology, and Early History of Citrus Research In California.* Oakland: Division of Agriculture and Natural Resources, 1989.

Lee, Beatrice Parson, *The History and Development of the Ontario Colony.* Thesis Presented to the Department of History, University of Southern California. Los Angeles, May 2, 1929.

Lothrop, Gloria Ricci. *Pomona: A Centennial History.* Chatsworth: Windsor Publications, Inc., 1988.

MacCurdy, Rahno Mabel. *The History of the California Fruit Growers Exchange.* Los Angeles, 1925.

McCrea, Janet M. *History of Chaffey College.* Undergraduate thesis, California State Polytechnic College. Pomona, 1971.

McWilliams, Carey. *Southern California Country: An Island On The Land.* New York: Duell, Sloan and Pearce, 1946.

Martz, Patricia. *Description and Evaluation of the Cultural Resources within Cucamonga, Demens, Deer and Hillside Creek Channels, San Bernardino and Riverside Counties, California.* Archaeological Research Unit, University of California, Riverside, UCARV No. 165, for US Army Corp of Engineers Environmental Planning Section. Los Angeles: US Army Corp of Engineers, 1976.

Ontario: A Compilation of Historical Articles and Booklets. Ontario Public Library.

Ontario Chamber of Commerce publications from the following years: 1947, 1949, 1957, 1961, 1966, 1970, 1974, 1976, 1979, 1984, 1986.

Ontario Chamber of Commerce Classification/Membership Directory, 1989.

Ontario Daily Report. Anniversary edition, November 7, 1937.

Ontario Daily Report. YesterYears, May 24, 1981.

Ontario Daily Report. 1917 Revisited, June 28, 1937.

Ontario: From A to Z. Local history scrap book. Ontario Public Library, Model Colony Room.

Ontario: George Chaffey's Model Colony. Articles from the *Ontario Herald*, 1937-1938. James Neill Northe, compiler.

Patterson, Tom. *A Colony for California: Riverside's First Hundred Years.* Riverside: Press-Enterprise Co., 1971.

————. "Santa Ana Wind Left It's Mark In Many A Year." Riverside: *The Press Enterprise*, December 11, 1988.

Peterson, P. Victor. *Native Trees of Southern California.* Berkeley, University of California Press, 1966.

Raven, Peter H. *Native Shrubs of Southern California.* Berkeley, University of California Press, 1966.

Rust, Irwin W. and Kelsey B. Gardner. *Sunkist Growers, Inc.: A California Adventure in Agricultural Cooperation.* Farmer Cooperative Service Circular 27. US Department of Agriculture, 1960.

San Bernardino County Sheriff's Department. "Drug Abuse is Life Abuse."

San Bernardino County Sun. Eight part series on development in the West End. September 10-17, 1989.

Schuling, Walter C. *San Bernardino County: Land of Contrasts.* Chatsworth: Windsor Publications, Inc., 1984.

The Sunkist Adventure. Farmer Cooperative Service Information 94. US Department of Agriculture, 1952.

Wright, Judy. *Claremont: A Pictorial History.* Claremont: Claremont Historic Resources Center, 1980.

Interviews

Kevin Bishop, *Ontario Daily Report*

C.C. "Kip" Carlson

Joan DeRyke, Dole Citrus

Bob Jackson, former director of redevelopment, City of Ontario

Richard "Bud" Novack, owner, Patton Sales Corp.

Michael O'Connor, assistant city manager, City of Ontario

Rick Starratt, San Antonio Orchards

Sue Sundell, Chaffey Joint Union High School District

Index